19 PRINCIPLES TO ACHIEVE LIFE SUCCESS

# THE
# BUMPY
# PATH TO
# FREEDOM

## DR. GUILLERMO CASTILLO

Foreword by Dr. John Demartini

Ultimate Publishing House

THE ULTIMATE PUBLISHING HOUSE (UPH)
Canadian Office: 205 Glen Shields Avenue
Toronto, Ontario,
Canada
L4K 2B0
Telephone: 647-883-1758

https://bumpypathtofreedom.com

www.ultimatepublishinghouse.com
E-mail: info@ultimatepublishinghouse.com

Quantity discounts are available on bulk purchases of this book for reselling, educational purposes, subscription incentives, gifts, sponsorship, or fundraising. Unique books or book excerpts can also be fashioned to suit special needs such as private labeling with your logo on the cover and a message from or a message printed on the second page of the book.

For more information, please contact our Special Sales Department at Ultimate Publishing House. Orders for a college textbook or course adoption use. Please contact Ultimate Publishing House Tel: 647-883-1758

THE BUMPY PATH TO FREEDOM
19 PRINCIPLES TO ACHIEVE LIFE SUCCESS
By: Dr. Guillermo Castillo

ISBN: 978-1-7354831-5-3

19 PRINCIPLES TO ACHIEVE LIFE SUCCESS

# THE
# BUMPY
# PATH TO
# FREEDOM

## DR. GUILLERMO CASTILLO

Foreword by Dr. John Demartini

# DEDICATION

This book is dedicated to the people who inspire me to be better every day. First and foremost, to my mother, who has been my hero and role model as a kind, compassionate, and incredibly giving human being. My mother is also the most resilient, persistent, and focused person I have encountered in my life. Without her guidance, I would be living a completely different life. To my father, who has provided balance, empathy, kindness, and loving support to me through every challenge in this life.

I dedicate this book to my two sons, who challenge me in every way. These two young men have taught me the value of patience and choosing my words with surgical precision. Their mother carried them for the first nine months of their lives, but it is I who have carried them since birth and will continue to do so for as long as I live. I feel I have known them long before they were born, and one of the major reasons I decided to write this book was to show them that it is possible to attack one's weaknesses head-on and come out better for it in the end.

I also dedicate this book to all the people who will remain nameless but were involved in all the experiences that are shared in this book and have ultimately contributed to creating the individual I am today. I especially dedicate this book to all those who tried to knock me down, suppress me, made me feel inadequate, called me stupid, and those who tried to bury me when my path no longer fulfilled their needs. It was all of you collectively that taught me the lessons I'm sharing that now give me so much strength.

# FOREWORD

Most people go through their life experiencing a journey of challenges that they may only later discover creates their unique path to freedom. What if you shifted your internal conversation about this journey starting now, and fully realized the many great opportunities it is providing? Dr. Castillo shares a compelling narrative of how he made it past those bumps in his life, which include life-altering hurdles in his personal life and formidable resistance in his career as a medical doctor. Through life's shakeups and the necessity for solutions, a new narrative emerged that has become a game-changer in his life. There is a resolution for every challenge you face in life that can take you a step closer to freedom—if you don't fear it that is, and you are ready to break past that which stands in your way. The path is bumpy, yet it is even more than joyfully rewarding!

This book is a guide for seeing the light. It is filled with practical strategies for mastering your life. Although the story and choices you may share and take can shift daily, they can now all become a source of inspiration. With these 19 Principles, Dr. Castillo has shared from his heart and showed how these principles encompass a life that you define as successful; a life in which you set the tone for a brighter and more inspiring world. Each of these 19 Principles helps you to unreel the root of your discontent and discover key components of your life that lead to peace of mind. The resolutions you need exist inside you right now; it's time to discover them and release your greatest and most empowered self.

Have you ever contemplated the possibility that you do already have the answers, but may be unaware of the inner strategy and methodology to unveil them? Your life journey and experiences are not good or bad, there are benefits and drawbacks to everything- it is all perception.

Through my years of writing books, speaking to international audiences, presenting seminars, and researching, I have realized many common threads between people from all corners of the world. There is a desire to reveal their highest, purest self, but there is also an unawareness of the specialized knowledge on how that really works. It sounds like a tall order, after all. So, when you come across someone who seems to have figured it out, you take notice.

People who draw you in due to their energy, inspiration, and authenticity are stand-outs in our world. They are the teachers, coaches, and mentors that shift the conversation and teach through their actions. Knowing that to be a truth, I also know that there is a reason that you've ended up with this book in front of you.

I share this with you because knowing this will provide an advantage to you, and now you have access to it in a way that can help you.

Dr. Castillo has created a transformation path using principles for great achievement based on his own achievements and journey through the "bumpy path". This book, which has resulted from Dr. Castillo's life lessons and observation reveals the keys to his and now your transformation. It is filled with great wisdom and inspiration. It will help you awaken to your inner "Why," your inspired calling, or your purpose, or whatever else you would love to call it. That's just the label, but what's inside of you, that's the real deal.

This type of inner self-discovery will be highly significant to you, regardless of your age or any situation in your life. It involves a deep knowing and greater understanding.

By reading Dr. Castillo's inspiring book you will enrich and empower your life. So savor each of its many insightful principles and ideas. If some seem a bit difficult to grasp at first, don't discredit them. Simply imbibe them and you will receive many transformative results. Commit to growing a greater understanding of what is happening in your mind and life. By doing so you will have already learned something of great value that will open your thoughts to an ever greater and bolder you.

Remember, you hold within the secret to your most inspiring and empowering achievements and your most empowered and fulfilling life.

Dr. John Demartini – International best-selling author of The Values Factor

www.drdemartini.com

# ACKNOWLEDGMENTS

First and foremost, I must thank my parents, not only for the obvious reasons, but for the sacrifices necessary to provide the environmental stressors I needed to ignite my fire. Knowingly and unknowingly, they are almost solely responsible for my indestructible sense of self . Without this strength, I would have never even dreamt of writing this book. They are the only example I know of two people creating a better whole. They are about to celebrate 50 years of marriage and are inseparable. They continue to inspire and give me hope.

There is also no way I could have achieved this goal in my life without my siblings who have been big motivational factors in all I do. Being a big brother is an enormous responsibility I took to heart. I was not a perfect big brother and, in many instances, failed to be the big brother they needed, but I did the best I could, and I did it for them.

The writing of this book began long before my two sons were even a thought, but it is they that are now at the core of my purpose. I am truly blessed to have been given the opportunity to raise these two young men. I always wanted two boys and could not have designed them better even if it was possible. Thank you for loving me and sharing this amazing experience we call life together.

Thank you to my best friend who has encouraged my crazy ideas and supported me in all my undertakings. She would have done things differently herself, but she stood with me regardless. In my life I have made thousands of acquaintances, but true friends I can count on one hand.

Thank you to Felicia and the UPH team for reaching out to me and pushing me to write this book. Thank you for listening to my stories and helping me make sense of the lessons I learned and can now share with the world. I hope this is the first book of many.

To everyone who contributed to my life experiences, positively or negatively, thank you for the life lessons and for helping me grow. Without all of you, I would not be the person I am today. Because of you, I have learned to navigate my bumpy path to freedom. I wish you this same freedom in your life.

# TABLE OF CONTENTS

# MY EVOLVING JOURNEY

"Everything on this earth is in
a continuous state of evolving,
refining, improving, adapting,
enhancing...changing. You were not
put on this earth to remain stagnant."

– STEVE MARABOLI

My parents' love for me was never in question, and for as long as I can recall, I knew they wanted better for me. They had hopes that I, along with my brother and sister, could move past a life of hard, backbreaking work, despite it being our passed-down tradition.

As migrant workers, my parents did all they could to help their family experience more. It had to be tough, tougher than anything I've ever faced as an adult, but I never doubted it existed. It was probably evidenced by me as a young boy when I asked my parents if we could stop returning to Mexico during the off-season of the rigorous agricultural work they did in California every year. I didn't want to get behind in school, and every time we left, I did. They decided to stay in the States and not take these well-deserved, hard-earned trips back to my birth place of Michoacan, Mexico.

My determination to work my way out of the agricultural farms and into something different was always present and was likely fueled by my mother. She spoke magical words to me that I took to heart, even if they were not completely true. She had a daily mantra she shared with me: "You are intelligent. You are strong. You are capable of anything you set your mind to." Those words inspire me to this day and, since they come from my mother, I take them as fact.

The life I know began with my parents' commitment to my life's opportunities. I knew I had to do the hard work, and they helped me. They never put tremendous pressure on me, only showing love and support, and today I see the immense satisfaction I have given them. It has been a journey of exploration, resilience, and now freedom.

**Every time I reflect on my life experiences, I can see the forces around me and from within me that have influenced the decisions in my life.**

Knowing where I come from is a fundamental part of understanding my life's voyage and how that little boy who could have landed as a farm worker in the fields of Monterey Bay, California, did not. Instead, I worked hard to have choices, such as the choice to attend the Keck School of Medicine at USC, one of the most prestigious medical schools in the world.

As I reflect on this boy, I see a path that hasn't always been easy or smooth. Parts of the journey had nearly broken me, but it is those struggles that I value the most. It is those tough times and mentally challenging experiences I endured that taught me the lessons that made me uniquely valuable and set me free. I now look forward to new challenges with excitement because I have the tools to grow through them and experience more joy and fulfillment every single day!

## THE LITTLE BOY FROM MICHOACAN, MEXICO

Some say the odds were stacked against me from the beginning. That is not what I say. Despite the hardships and low expectations for me, I had no problems working hard to make my American dream come to fruition. I knew I was fortunate enough that my parents did not want me to go to school only until I met the legal age requirements to enter the workforce. In our culture it was custom that children would enter the labor force as teenagers and begin a life in the fields earning money to help support the family.

We lived in the small town of Watsonville, nestled in a corner on the border of Monterey and Santa Cruz counties. Our even smaller community within this coastal town consisted of many families, most of which were close relatives of one another, that worked the fields. The land we lived on and that my parents farmed totaled about 100 acres, and it was beautiful! It consisted of rolling hills filled with strawberries, raspberries, and apples. The small cabins we lived in were built within the fields, and it was all owned by a very kind Japanese gentleman who charged only seven dollars a week for rent as long as someone in the family worked for him. As a kid, I found this setting to be perfect because it offered the freedom to roam about safely yet remain close to my parents, who were out in the fields "earning a living."

I have a cousin who says that we were all poor but didn't know it. Truer words have never been spoken of my humble childhood environment. We were all in the same position. When you're surrounded by those who have so little, even for basic needs, but have a lot of love and community, it is easier to manage. I am in no way implying that money is not important. I love the freedom that money provides, but when I reflect on those simpler days, it reminds me that material possessions and our attachment to them would have taken away some of those moments that made my childhood feel so amazingly complete.

In time, as I grew into my own, I realized that I am a combination of traits from both my mother and father. My dad gave me his calmness, and even under extreme pressure, I can stay calm, rationalize, and react positively. From my mother and her mother, I received my drive and motivation. The drive these women instilled in me, and the calm, collected safety my father provided, have freed me to take chances. Failures, and I have had many, have knocked me down but NEVER for long because I always knew that I had a home where I was loved and supported unconditionally.

When I was a child, and until I was a teenager, I believed my parents to be superhuman. Surprise—they were human like everyone else. Go figure! That truth did not mean I couldn't respect them or admire them for their own unique strengths. One of the biggest lessons they taught me, and I admire to this day, is one I don't feel they intentionally recognize: they are living their truth. Within their realm of possibilities, they understand and accept their roles in this life. They know exactly who they are, and in sharing that with the world, they allow others to be themselves as well. Some chose tougher paths, like my brother, who has had problems that led to early fatherhood, selling drugs, prison time, and all the chaos that comes along with that. He is someone who heard the same encouraging words and could count on the same support as I did from our parents but chose a completely different path. My sister is nearly fifteen years younger than me so when I left my parents' home for college, she was only 3 years old, but it has been a joy to get to know her as a young woman. She has lived with me for the last six years and helps me raise my sons with the same love and traditions that our parents enriched our childhood with.

These people, who they were, and who they have become, make up my family. None of us are perfect; we all have challenges, and it's exciting to see how we are all doing the best we can to make the most out of our lives.

As I think back, I can only smile at some of the lovely memories that came from being around great people. One of those fond memories is of the ice cream truck that we would hear coming from a mile away. Its distinct music would stop us dead in our tracks no matter what we were doing and have us running to it with abandon. The other heart-warming memory is the Mexican sweet bread truck, which came to our secluded farm twenty miles outside of town every Saturday. My grandpa would always be waiting with a dollar to give us so we could enjoy that delicious bread as we walked home with our parents from their Saturday's work in the field. It was a special time filled with love and laughter.

Another life-altering moment in my life was when my parents saved up enough money to buy a small house in town. I was nine years old, and it felt so scary to leave our little world on the farm despite the excitement of owning our own home. For my parents, it must have been terrifying—they were going from seven dollars a week rent on the farm to a $500/month mortgage. The bank didn't care that my parents' work was seasonal. They wanted their monthly mortgage payments the first of every month year-round, work or no work!

The move was eye-opening in more ways than I had imagined. I was thrown into a new environment where the financial disparity between my family and our new neighbors was obvious. My neighbors tter educated, had well-paying jobs, took summer vacations, and were even able to take time off work to attend their kids' sporting events at school. My parents were always working, so I couldn't have many of those experiences.

These new surroundings opened my eyes to new possibilities that I absorbed and felt compelled to achieve. I loved my parents, but I wanted what my neighbors had, maybe even more. It was around this time that my parents were abruptly forced to change their long-term plans as well. The Mexican peso crashed, leaving many people who sent money back to Mexico broke, and of course, my parents were included in this group. This was the moment when my parents' dream of returning to Mexico ended. They saw our family's future was in the United States, so they pivoted and were able to make a good life here. The same was not true for other migrant farm workers with different mindsets.

**My parents' resolve taught me resilience, and I sure needed it to commit to my studies and start to pave the path to my future—my bumpy path to freedom.**

## FINDING MY CALLING

When I said I was a big dreamer, I meant it. My childhood dream was to become an astronaut, but that career path was ultimately not in the cards for me. I somehow ended up being the only member of my family to be nearsighted and require corrective glasses. That immediately eliminated me from ever being a pilot. So, like my parents, I had to pivot. I could have gone into computer technology on a full scholarship because I excelled at math, but that path didn't excite me at all. I nearly chose that path only because it came with a full scholarship, but once again my dad came through and encouraged me to follow my dreams as he assured me the money was meaningless in the long run.

I ended up at UC Davis, the top nutrition science university in the country, as a nutrition science major. I did very well in college and was on a direct path toward my goal of completing a PhD in Nutrition Science so that I could help combat childhood obesity. Sounds like a great career, but along my path I was once again encouraged to pivot. My mentor, who was a National Institutes of Health (NIH) inductee as a nutrition scientist, pulled me aside and said, "Guillermo, you are a people person. You will not be happy in a lab. You would be of better service as a medical doctor helping people face to face." He made sense but I was unsure, so I applied to graduate school for both nutrition science and medicine. It was not easy, but I did get into medical school, surprisingly more than one, despite the discouraging words of my college counselor who was positive I was not a candidate for a US medical school and should apply in Mexico. When I received my acceptance into the Keck School of Medicine at USC, my decision was made; I would pursue a career in medicine and become a doctor.

Despite the intensive hard work and rigor of medical school, by year three I was uncertain if I had made the right choice. The business of medicine was changing dramatically, and I did not like what doctors were being trained to do. It wasn't what I had envisioned, but $180,000 in student debt compelled me to see it through. After a lot of bumps and hurdles, I realized that being a doctor did NOT fulfill me, nor did it define who I was as a person. It did, however, gain me credibility and open doors. It also allowed me to forge long-lasting working relationships that I still leverage today in my journey to help as many people as I can. It took me fifteen years to finally conclude that being a traditional medical doctor was not my life's work, but that I could instead redirect my course and find joy in everything I do.

Clarity of purpose has finally entered my life, and it has changed everything. I am certain you can relate. You've had challenges in your pursuits—I am sure of it—and have had decisions forced upon you that you had to deal with. You may still be in the midst of this transition or shift. You may be looking for something to help guide your decisions or simply reassure you that you are deserving of all that joy and freedom you desire. Maybe you are as unsure as I was that you have what you need to make your hopes and dreams come true. I hope this book will show you how to evaluate those experiences and leverage them to realize your unique value and ultimately find and fulfill your calling. I am so full of joy and love now that I seek for opportunities to positively impact others professionally and personally. I hope that by the time you finish this book, you will feel the same way.

## SEIZE YOUR DAY

Today, it is my joy and responsibility to help my sons become men who find their own journeys and grow into their own personal truths. Becoming a father made it clear to me that this privilege is a blessing and that my priority is to guide my sons to become better men than I could ever be. They are clearly better humans already, and I cannot wait to see what an incredible impact they will have on this world.

Their upbringing is so different from mine. They have not lived in a world where they want for anything. Knowing this, it is important to create a hunger in them that leads to a drive that achieves their own aspirations.

**It's not bad to want to give your kids everything you didn't have, so long as you don't forget to give them what you did have.**

It was almost my forty-third birthday when I awoke one day and realized I'd had enough! Enough of fulfilling others' expectations of me. Enough of measuring my success by the material possessions I was acquiring. Enough of playing a role in a medical system that was not aligned with my own morals and beliefs. I would NOT continue to compromise who I knew myself to be any longer to fit into an image that I believed the world expected to see!

I had success—by how others often define it—but I did not have happiness or fulfillment. I felt like I was dying inside a little bit by not living true to myself. The problem suddenly became that I didn't know who, exactly, the person I believed myself to be was any longer. I had been living this life and willfully ignoring my internal objections for so many years that I didn't know where to begin. It was not until I embarked on a long-overdue journey of deep introspective searching and exploring that I was able to remember the essence of my core beliefs, morals, strengths, and most importantly, where my values comes from and why the world needs them. All those strengths were based on my experiences, and today I realize that. I'm finally living free, having navigated the bumpiest part on that path to freedom.

I am living my truth.

I know without wavering who I am.

I know my value and why the world needs me.

I know what I want my legacy to be.

Being aligned emotionally, mentally, and physically has become my reality. I feel good about everything I am involved in, and everything I do is an act of love.

I make connections everywhere I go because I genuinely care about everyone I interact with. I have learned how to live without judgment, and I don't give advice. What I am willing to do is share what life has taught me through lessons and experiences. Helping others extract lessons from those defining moments has now become a passion for me.

**Every day I am grateful for life. I breathe in the fresh air.
I live every moment of every day with purpose, and I**

**see opportunities to positively impact those around me.
Today, it is easy to be grateful for my blessings.**

We are all constantly learning and evolving, especially if we are living our best life. Our perspectives change as our wisdom and insight grow. This is how we define our own value and understand where it comes from as well. It is imperative that we continue to keep an open mind and recognize when our world—or the universe—is showing us a better way. Feeling strong in your beliefs and knowing you have the tools to successfully take on any challenge that comes your way gives you the energy and enthusiasm to face the unknown that tomorrow brings.

I am not saying that everything always goes as planned or that all turns out well. I am not saying every day is happiness. What I am saying is that I no longer ask the universe to spare me from these challenges, but instead I ask for the strength to face them head-on. I can feel good about this because I find joy even in the challenging days when things just don't go my way.

My ego is in check because I am aware that it is protective of me and wants to help me avoid pain. That sounds like a good deal on the surface, but it truly comes at a bitter price. The ego also keeps you from seeing your faults, displaying the humility to accept a better way, taking on challenges, and especially from challenging your current beliefs. Being aligned allows you to look past the ego. It is only then that you can see the real you—faults, defects, imperfections, weaknesses, and all. It can absolutely be terrifying, but it can also be brilliant and liberating. It is the path to freedom.

Look, I don't have it all figured out; I am on a constant journey of learning and self-exploration. The best definition of success I have ever heard is "success is the progressive realization of an ideal goal." The key word here is "ideal" because that "ideal" should be unattainable and, therefore, a lifelong journey. My hope is that as you read this book, it infuses your heart with your desire to go on a journey of self-discovery through applying the 19 Principles for life that I am sharing. Each one is meant to be evaluated to determine how it applies to you so you can better understand why you are here, who you are, and what the possibilities of your reality are. My hope is that by the end of this book, you will be on a path of discovery. Every day forward will become an exciting adventure and opportunity to share your value with the world. The world needs you now more than ever.

# FINDING THE HIDDEN ORDER OF YOUR CHAOS

"It's all about finding the calm in the chaos."

– DONNA CARON

The narratives that we allow into our minds have a tremendous impact on what we experience and feel. Our outcomes are defined by what we allow to fester within us.

As I look back at my brother and his life's journey, I can see this point demonstrated quite clearly today. I am more aware of it now than I was at the time it was happening.

For many years I carried a great emotional burden! I felt responsible for many of my little brother's challenges in life. His experiences in this life have been so very different from mine, and the possibility that I had been responsible for his hardships haunted me. How could I feel such a responsibility, you might ask. There was a moment during a confrontation with my brother where he directly blamed me for his choices. Those who know me would tell you I am not the most sensitive of people but coming from my brother whom I love dearly made it impossible not to take it to heart. He said, "You set the bar too high. I could never be you so I did everything I could to be the opposite of you." He is only three years younger than I and we grew up in a very small farm town. That meant that we shared the same teachers in school and coaches in sports. It is unfair but reasonable that those teachers and coaches expected him to be just like me. By no means was I a perfect child, but I was a teacher's pet in school and excelled in sports. My brother, on the other hand, was and is a rebellious free spirit who thrives on challenging authority.

It was punishingly painful to consider that what I thought was "setting a good example," or "paving the way," impeded my little brother from shining as an individual. Had I played a role in shaping his decisions and therefore pushed him to becoming a father at such a young age, going to prison for selling drugs, and feeling as unworthy as he did for so many years? For a long time, I believed this, and it made me feel horrible. He was family, not an unknown stranger, and feeling that I had made his life tougher made me feel like I had failed as a big brother.

All this emotion and resentment existed, both inside my brother and within me. Only he can lay testimony to how he dealt with what troubled him. I had to dig deep and take a very introspective look through my intentions and chosen paths. I was forced to journey into my heart and soul to determine if what my brother suggested was true. Even more importantly, if there was any truth in his words, how would I respond? I felt certain that there was a solution that didn't have to make one of us a winner and the other a loser. We could both be better.

Through this challenge, I learned that the chaos this situation induced within me was of my own doing. I did not have to take my brother's accusations personally. I could have instead chosen to view them objectively. This could have allowed me **to avoid** the emotional distress and therefore enable me to extract the value embedded within such insight. That kind of emotional maturity would have helped me be more present for my brother as a source of strength during his most difficult times. In my family, being the oldest means I am the strong one that is supposed to help all others, and in this case I failed miserably. I did learn, through this experience, that my value only comes forth if I can calm the inner chaos, acknowledge yet move past my emotions, and ultimately maintain logic and reasoning. When I am capable of this the results for me and all involved are extraordinary.

Evaluating your emotional house is not an easy task. It takes time and can feel painful because you are exposing your vulnerabilities and insecurities. In my case, I couldn't control how or why my brother made his decisions. I had no impact on the outcomes. He was going to be compared to me regardless of anything he or I could do. All I could do was continue to demonstrate my love for him whether he accepted it as genuine or not. I had to learn to find inner peace even when my brother refused my love and questioned my intentions.

"When the chaos creates comfort, and the pain stops hurting your head, when you learn to accept the whole world, you know you possess yourself."

– ANI SHAVERDYAN

Sometimes it is easier to ignore the hurt and the chaos, but unresolved pain will have to surface in time. It is only surrender to the pain and acceptance of the chaos that allowed me to finally see that I had done all I could for myself and my family. By knowing that I was being the best version of myself and therefore the best example for my brother the pain subsided, and my own inner order gave me peace of mind.

Today, I see that my pathway to success did not come at the price of my brother's well-being. Not only was my success an invitation for his own, but as his older brother, I had pioneered a trustworthy roadmap for him to follow. As soon as I could accept that my success was well deserved and accept my brother's chosen path led him in the opposite direction, the pain that intensified as we grew distant stopped impacting my own satisfaction.

Those moments where you have self-doubt, which everyone does at times, are the best opportunities to revisit your own acceptance. You don't have to meet anyone else's expectations of you, instead accept what you are and allow that to be your inner peace. When your own narrative isn't serving you, change it. Listen to your intuition and settle the chaos brewing inside of you.

## REFLECTIVE EXERCISE

Finding ways to move past the chaos that impedes revealing your better self is the goal here. You must get comfortable with self-acceptance. Considering that your inner voice could be wrong is the first step in that direction. There is no shame in this process, as it is an essential part of the path to freedom.

> **When the heart reconciles itself with the mind, you have put at least one element of your chaos to rest. You have prepared yourself for the next step.**

This process is how you get to know your truth. Use the insights that come with reconciliation to identify the areas in your life that create challenges for you.

You can identify these areas by recognizing when what you present to the world outwardly conflicts with what you feel inwardly.

- Do I feel good about what I am portraying outwardly?
- Do I have doubts? If so, about what exactly?
- Are these doubts self-inflicted or am I punishing myself for not meeting others' expectations?
- Do I accept myself wholeheartedly? And am I sharing my true self with the world?
- I can only control myself, so how can I change my inner narrative to calm the chaos and optimize my inner peace?

Lying takes a lot of energy—even lying to yourself—and that is energy that is taken away from finding your authentic self and tapping into the freedom that comes with self-acceptance.

* * *

The more I have gotten to understand and accept who and what I am, the freer I have become from the chaos that stifles my curiosity and stunts my growth.

# DISCIPLINE GETS RESULTS

"The great master key to riches is nothing more or less than the self-discipline necessary to help you take full and complete possession of your own mind."

– NAPOLEON HILL

How do I go from doing what I have trained for my entire life to a new path where uncertainty was the only feeling that was assured every day? I survived my medical education almost entirely due to a voracious hunger to improve my family's socioeconomic and financial future. I entered the workforce as a doctor with the same hunger and therefore made myself available for all work that came my way. For 15 years I never turned down a patient or opportunity to work. That meant my phone was on 24/7 and I am not exaggerating when I tell you I couldn't go five minutes without a call or a text message related to work. So, when I abruptly decided to make a turn and change career paths, I faced one of my toughest challenges.

Instantly my phone went silent! You may think that is a blessing, but for my entire career the phone ringing meant I was needed and therefore I was making money. Now when suddenly NO ONE, and I mean NO ONE was looking for me, fear was the overwhelming response. I would check my phone every five minutes to make sure it was still on and send test messages to make sure my cell service was ok. The quiet that I so desired was daunting when I suddenly found it.

The best way to quiet the fear was to focus on my daily tasks. Everything I worked on daily was to further my education and value so that I could truly serve others and help them meet their health goals. The progress was not clear at all and some days I was sure that I was regressing not progressing. Acceptance was slow, but after a couple of weeks (could have been months!) I was able to get in a good flow and make daily progress toward redefining my purpose and find joy in that process. Sounds easy, doesn't it? Wish I could tell you it was, but like most things worth writing about it was NOT EASY. Day after day I had to convince myself I was doing the right thing and that the journey was my goal.

**Success, after all, is the progressive realization of an ideal goal!**

After months of disciplined work, I began to see positive changes in myself and my clients. Some days were difficult, and some were great, but what I can tell you is that just before bed every night I would get this overwhelming feeling of peace and gratitude. It was those days that helped me believe in the process and propelled me ahead day after day.

**You can't be something in one aspect of your life and something different elsewhere.**

This means that you can start practicing the art of discipline in any aspect of your life. This is a very important point because it means that you can choose the one thing that means the most to you or maybe is easiest to attack. For you it could be becoming a present and involved parent, or maybe the best leader at your company, or simply getting in the best physical health of your life.

My discipline first developed in the gym! I started going to the gym at age 14. Getting up at 4 am wasn't easy but because I wasn't old enough to join a gym on my own, I had to go with my uncle and that was his gym time. That 4am wake-up call has found me tired and sore beyond belief many times, but I still get up, and the closer I get to the gym, the more energized I become. The results in the gym were not always obvious and at times I felt like the pictures of the bodybuilders I would admire in fitness magazines were fake! There were many times when I didn't feel like working out, but as, a chubby kid I wanted nothing more than to be the best version of myself possible and working out was the only way to balance my voracious love of food. I had to learn how to trust the process and develop unwavering discipline. Day after day, and year after year I continue to get up early in the morning and make it to the gym. To this day this is my practice. In fact, most days by the time I am completely awake I am already at the gym.

This mentality and persistence translated directly to school, sports, and every project I have taken on. It is only because of this focused practice of discipline that I excelled in high school, college, medical school, and all my endeavorsthereafter. I survived my medical residency and 21 years of this incredibly demanding career not because I was the smartest but because I had the discipline to keep working towards my goal one day at a time day after day.

**It was necessary to tap into the discipline to stick with what I inherently believed was a better and more fulfilling life.**

Demonstrating discipline is not always exciting or glamorous, but, in time, it always provides results . I have had to learn this the hard way. Multiple failures clearly taught me that "easy come easy go." Every time I made the choice for immediate gratification and an easy win, things fell apart just as quickly as they came together. What makes discipline so difficult to adopt is that it requires the daily practice of the most mundane and routine tasks over and over again. The truly successful keep going until the goal is accomplished. How long does that take? Sometimes it is forever, but when the goal is worthwhile forever is not long enough! One of the most important choices you can make about practicing discipline is deciding to be fascinated and obsessed with **the process or accepting that you will be bored out of your mind from the** disciplined tasks long before any evidence of its benefits. There is rarely any dopamine rush that fills you with euphoria. There is no big reward at the end of every day. There is only a sense of strength and reliability in trusting that your actions are leading you down the best path.

**It's not what you get from disciplined actions, it is what you become that matters most!**

Discipline must be a pillar of your philosophy! It requires many small, sometimes seemingly insignificant actions that lead to a compounding effect over time. Often, it is only in retrospect that you can appreciate the results. Being disciplined creates a reputation and legacy to be proud of. You will become someone who finishes everything you start. You will be known, most importantly to yourself, as someone who shows up no matter what. You will attack all challenges with abandon because you will never doubt your ability to work until the job is done.

Discipline becomes easier when you find a way to incorporate something you look forward to in that daily grind. You will have to learn to trust the process and pat yourself on the back at day's end.

## "TRUE FREEDOM IS IMPOSSIBLE WITHOUT A MIND MADE FREE BY DISCIPLINE"

### – MORTIMER J ADLER

It sounds almost counterintuitive, but discipline is the path to freedom. An important part of discipline is also deciding what NOT to work on or who not to work with. Not everyone who needs your help deserves it. In my life, I have found many interesting people and projects that needed my help, and when I was younger, I just couldn't say NO. As you can likely conclude, my inability to make the most important tasks the priority disrupted my discipline and therefore created turmoil in my consciousness. This disruption led to erratic busy work that did not lead to linear progress in any of my goals.

The more honest I was with myself the easier it became to attain the determination necessary to maintain my discipline. I learned that I could not try to live up to someone else's expectations. It was only when I was clear about my own vision and personal goals that an obsessively disciplined approach led me toward this extraordinary alignment and sense of freedom.

## REFLECTIVE EXERCISE

Discipline is something that you want to practice all 24 hours of the day. Sounds overwhelming? It's really not. I say 24 hours because being disciplined about your sleep is essential to your health and necessary to optimize your days. You need to rest and recover optimally in order to give your best every day. Be very honest with yourself and decide what path you want to be on.

1. Establish a plan and some loose boundaries that grant you permission to have some laxity in the path you follow. Sometimes the best ideas and strides come from a mind that thinks less rigidly.
2. Set the parameters each day for what you need to get done and assign a certain period of time to complete them. Note: for some people, the word daily throws them off from attaining a goal because it seems cumbersome; find a way to make daily not seem like such an inhibiting word.

Just know that when a goal is not written down it does become easier to stop working on it. This is why your self-set aspirations need to be around you everywhere—in writing, on your phone, on your computer, as your bookmark for the book you're reading, and so on. Keep a list of your goals in sight so they remain relevant to you.

It may seem unstimulating to spend time focused on discipline, but by embracing it, you are taking a significant step toward the ultimate goal of freedom. Once the discipline is there, freedom will follow as the reward to it. Take a few moments to reflect on these questions:

1. Why am I working on this goal? Is it my passion or someone else's expectation?

2.     Am I making the most important things my priority? If not, how can I remove distractions?
3.     How often should I measure progress? Remember progress has to be measured in reasonable time increments.
4.     How do my goals positively affect my loved ones? Does this increase my determination and drive?
5.     If I accomplish my goal, how will my life and those around me be affected? Let this fuel your resolve.

When you learn the value of discipline, you will have found the tenacity you need to achieve just about any goal you set your mind to, personal or professional.

\*    \*    \*

DO NOT lose sight of your why! Disciplined action without direction for the sake of being busy will NOT get you to your desired destination. You need to know precisely what you are pursuing!

# DEVELOP A MINDSET OF POSSIBILITIES

"Our aspirations are
our possibilities."

– SAMUEL JOHNSON

Have you ever known someone that is so fixed in their mindset that arguments are futile? Do you know entire communities that are this way?

The family and community I was born into had mindsets just like that, FIXED and UNWAVERING. Everyone was expected to fall into line. Once a person was legally old enough to join the workforce, they would quit school and get a job to help support the family. Then, as they had families, the process would repeat itself. Looking back, I can see why this tradition was upheld and rarely questioned. The families worked long and hard for the harvesting season of May through October, but from mid-October until April, they lived like royalty in Mexico and enjoyed a lot of quality time together. Those memories created back in their hometown were priceless. I can also look back and tell you that the drawback is there was no progress in that process as a long-term plan.

How I did not end up with that same fate is almost miraculous. As you read already in this book, I have an extraordinary mother! My mother brainwashed me in the most loving and positive ways! You may think that sounds horrible, so a bit of an explanation is in order. From the time I was born, I have memories of my mother repeating in my ear that I should not follow in her footsteps. I heard day in and day out that I was capable of anything I set my mind to. I was told daily that I was smart, handsome, brilliant, and so on. While these suggestions were by no means fact and exclusively my mom's point of view, they left a great impression on me. I was convinced that I was in control of my own fate, and my mom's words encouraged me to be limitless.

Because no one in our family had ever completed more than a grade school education, my mother's goal for me was to complete a four-year college education. She did not influence my actual career path, but her intention was that my value would come from my mind and not my physical abilities as those would fail as I got older. Her secondary intention was that I become the example for those who would follow behind me in our family and prove to them that incredible opportunities lie beyond the world we knew as seasonal farm laborers in the fields. Most importantly, my mother wanted me to never feel less than anyone else on this planet and the only equalizer in her eyes was education. What amazing vision this woman had especially for being so young and coming from such an oppressed origin.

For those of you who don't have an incredible mother to plant suggestions like these in your head, you can still positively "brainwash" yourself. How is this possible? Whether you are aware of it or not, you have a narrative about yourself in your subconscious that dictates how you see yourself and therefore how you act and make decisions. Turns out we become what we think about all day long. It is our own responsibility to focus on positives and self-growth and let go of our self-defeating negative chatter. Our self-talk determines how we see ourselves and, therefore, how we act in any situation that may arise. The message should be positive, especially when you seek results of that nature. We seem to encounter many obstacles because, for reasons we aren't always aware of, many of us are riddled with negativity. What I suggest is not easy, but changing how you perceive yourself and therefore how you treat and act for yourself is the only way forward. As we discussed in Principle 2: Discipline Gets Results, this self-talk must be daily practice until you believe the new narrative. It took my mother years of daily affirmations to get me to believe!

> "I believe that love is the choice we make to raise ourselves
> and others to the highest planes of existence."
>
> – RICHARD PAUL EVANS

No matter how loving and encouraging these words can be or who is the one voicing them, you have a role to play in accepting or rejecting them on your path to betterment. Most people reject kind and encouraging words even from their parents; just tuning them out for reasons I will never fully understand. To me, they felt like a gift, and I embraced the responsibility that gift implied. Maybe therein lies the problem, believing in yourself means you must then live up to that potential. We all know that it is easier to take the path of least resistance than it is to try so hard and "fail" at being great.

**I could have doubted my mother's affirmations and instead believed others who told me I was an idiot, an incapable person, and a dreamer.**

It saddens me to know that so many of the people I grew up with chose to fall in line with lives that I do not feel were indicative of their true potential. My high school counselor advised me to become a "lemon picker," and my college advisor strongly recommended I apply to medical school in Mexico because "Unites States medical schools would never accept you with your grades." During my residency training, I was asked if I was "stupid or just didn't read."

It is shameful what adults in authority positions say and do to kids that severely impact their trajectory. I will never forget a kid who grew up next door to me and was only a year behind me in school. We used to play together in the neighborhood and our parents were friends. As I remember this boy was pretty much normal as a kid, but he struggled in school. I recall trying to help him with schoolwork and trying to teach him to tie his shoes with little success, he just did not learn in the traditional manner. I really liked him as a friend, so I didn't mind trying to help. I will never forget the day I heard his own father spoke of his son's "lack of intelligence." My mom picked us up from school one day as parent-teacher conferences were approaching. This is where our teachers would give firsthand reports of our accomplishments and progress in school to our parents. This boy's teacher mentioned to my mom that she was excited to meet his parents and find a way to help him get up to speed. When my mom delivered the message to his father, his response was heartbreaking: "they'll just tell me my son is a dummy and can't learn; we're just waiting for when he's old enough to legally quit school and work in the fields." The dad said this in front of the boy! I can only imagine the damage hearing that caused in that boy. That was his messaging, his brainwashing, and as far as I know, that boy fulfilled his father's prophesy. He accepted those words as truth and lived out that limited potential.

**When we think of our possibilities for life, we must realize that rarely is someone born with the right mindset; it must be developed.**

Do you ever think that the universe is against you? You were born into the wrong family, the wrong socioeconomic group, or the wrong era? Taxes are too high? There is no opportunity for a person like yourself? If you were smarter, you would have been a lawyer, doctor, or engineer? It is easier to blame others or our environment for our lack of accomplishments rather than ourselves. The truth is very few people are born into all the right circumstances. Those who succeed in life create the circumstances that favor them in any environment. I am not saying this is an easy thing to do, but success stories of people doing this are out there. Unless they are a Thomas

Edison or even a Sir Richard Branson (who had a similar story), we often don't read about them.

If you feel stuck in an unfavorable environment or even just a bad mindset, remember that there is no law that says you cannot overcome those. In fact, the opposite is true. Life seems to give you exactly what you deserve. Deserving health, love, riches, and success is completely up to you. In life, you get what you give. I know what you are thinking. "How do I give what I don't have?" Opening your mind and believing in yourself is the starting point down a new path to something incredibly purposeful.

## REFLECTIVE EXERCISE

To find out where you are with your mindset and the possibilities you have set for yourself, you must reflect deeply on your perception of your life and its many possibilities. Find a quiet and reflective place to ponder these questions or even meditate on them. Spending some time with yourself to determine what your dreams are, which ones you wish to pursue, and how to go about doing so, is time well spent. It is the spark which will ignite the embers of your greatest potential. Start with these reflections:

- What is it that you believe about yourself that dictates your mindset?
- Where does this narrative come from?
- Are your beliefs based on what you've been told you are or what you've determined you are?
- Do your beliefs about your potential and opportunity serve you well?
- Are your actions rooted in what you believe or just a habit you've been trained to follow?

After this reflection, take action.

1. What would you replace your current narrative with?
2. Start acting like the person you want to be and keep doing it until you become that exactly!
3. Start to view yourself differently every day, and at day's end, acknowledge and affirm these positive shifts in your narrative.
4. Start aligning your thoughts and actions with the person you are becoming.
5. Pick an interval of time, maybe weekly to start then monthly, to evaluate progress and allow for pivot when necessary.

# FIND DIGNITY IN A GREAT DAY'S WORK

"The dignity is in the worker, not the job."

– HOWARD FAST

Adulting sucks! When I was a kid all the adults around me worked long hard hours six to seven days a week. I can't say for certain that any of them liked the work, per se, but what was obvious was that they had pride in the work they did. The work of a farmer is backbreaking and never ending, but there was dignity in providing a good day's labor for a wage. I recall sitting on the porch of our little house, where my parents and grandparents would take off their muddy work shoes before entering the house. Dad and grandpa sharing how sore their backs were and how much their feet and hands hurt! I asked why they wouldn't get a different job that was less physical and paid more money. I will never forget their answer. Both said the same thing with different words. To paraphrase the answer was: We aren't qualified or skilled in anything else. We also love to see the product of our labor at the end of the day. There is a lot of value in making an honest living and the peaceful sleep hard physical labor evokes is priceless.

As a kid, I didn't think much about it, but now as a responsible parent myself I understand the effort and sacrifice my parents exerted with honor for our family. Each day began at 5am picking berries in the fields and did not end until they had fed us dinner and prepared the household for the next day's duties. I know this was not an easy task to maintain for so many years, yet they did not complain. Honestly, I cannot imagine working fourteen to sixteen hours straight, tending to all the household chores, and giving three kids the attention we needed every single day. Even more amazingly, they did it all with pride. It is a blessing the work is seasonal, and the winters are spent recovering in Mexico.

**Dignity is a presence you exude that shows you are willing to step up to the life presented to you and give it your best, even when it is not "ideal."**

As amazing as I have always known my parents to be, it is the dignity with which they accepted and handled their lives which is most admirable. My mother shared many times that her dreams were much greater than her reality but reinforced that this was not my destiny. There is great dignity in all work regardless of what it entails. If your purpose is to be a septic tank cleaner and you are the best possible septic tank cleaner you could be then you are dignified and should be proud. My dad's jobs, and he's had many over the years, were all physically demanding and always required long hours. To this day he takes pride in not missing a day and performing to the best of his ability. One of his companies recognized him for not missing a single day of work in ten seasons! I knew there were times when he was sick or tired or even mentally exhausted, yet he never allowed those feelings to trump his commitment to the job. I know now that he also has a very strong belief that he is a guy that doesn't ever quit and sees everything through no matter what!

The topic of dignity cannot be discussed without having a special call-out to my mother, as well. She was nonstop with her days. Not only did she work all day, then come home and tend to her family and do most of the cooking (Dad cooked sometimes), but she had to tend to all the other tasks at the house. Sundays were laundry and grocery shopping days. My mom somehow made it fun. We would pack the car early with all our laundry and supplies and take the twenty to thirty minute drive into town. Our first stop was church of course - I grew up in a very catholic family. Directly after church service, we would go to the laundromat to tend to that cumbersome task. After laundry, we would pick up a bucket of KFC (fried chicken for those who are not familiar) and go to the park for a picnic and playtime! For my brother and I, this was our favorite part of every Sunday. Our very last task before heading home to prepare for Monday morning was grocery shopping. Since we could only do this once a week, it was quite exciting to see the refrigerator full of food again- especially for a chubby kid who was always hungry! Even on her one day off my mother worked hard to provide for us.

In our culture, the men handled the things that had to do with mechanics, carpentry, and tasks like that. How to manage a household, cook, and provide a rich environment for my kids I learned from my mother. This came in handy when I found myself a single dad when my boys were only one and three years old. I handled the role of mom and dad the best I could and took pride in my efforts. I feel fortunate that I grew up with a strong female figure and didn't feel encumbered by society's inflicted gender-specific roles.

**"No work is insignificant. All work that uplifts humanity has dignity."**

**– MARTIN LUTHER KING**

I recall an interesting story with my sons when they were only four and six years old. It was a Saturday morning and we had just finished eating breakfast when I excused myself so I could get to the hospital and see my patients. My oldest son quickly said, "Oh come on Dad, I thought we were going to play now. It's Saturday, why do you have to work on a weekend?" I replied, "Well, don't you want to eat on Saturday?" Of course, he did, and he said so. It took me a minute to reflect on my answer and soon realized that the lesson I wanted to cement was that my work was important, and I had people counting on me to help them feel better. I wanted them to understand I had chosen a career that requires sacrifice as do all careers dedicated to the betterment of people. One of the sacrifices I was happy to make, was working on some weekends even if it meant I couldn't play with my sons all day. I reverted to what I learned as a child from my parents. Helping others was my job and doing it to the best of my ability has always provided me with a sense of dignity, and this is a valuable lesson that I have emphasized to my sons.

Dignity from work is something that is at risk today, I feel. Social media is full of people that portray very lavish lifestyles that, at least superficially, are earned without hard work or education. There is minimal high-value content available for kids on the internet that emphasizes the hard work and daily grind it takes to reach worthwhile goals. I have heard my own kids and their friends say many times, "I don't need school. I can be a YouTuber, a gamer, or a professional athlete." Far too few people know the stories of discipline, perseverance and hard work developed over many years that preceded the success and glory of these public figures we admire. Dignity, however, does not come from making a lot of money or being famous. Dignity is born from the knowledge that we give everything of ourselves in every job, task, or project we commit to.

**Hard work does not always lead to success or even progress.**

You cannot let yourself grow distracted with busy work. The work you spend your time on must be focused and directed toward your goals. I spent years lost and unfulfilled making a living but feeling like I was spinning my wheels. I found little dignity in work without meaningful progress toward my goal of freedom. On the contrary, without realizing it, busy meaningless work slowly stripped away my dignity and left me feeling defeated. It did not matter how much "stuff" I accumulated because all those things were symbolic handcuffs. That "stuff" required me to keep doing the same busy work that was not serving me only to maintain the "stuff" that did not enrich my life. Making progress toward freedom required sacrificing that "stuff", but in the end provided me with a dignity in my work that is priceless.

## REFLECTIVE EXERCISE

Having dignity begins with not allowing yourself to be distracted from the work necessary to make progress toward your ideal goals. Take some time to think about what you spend most of your days doing:

- Are you clear about your ideal goals?
- Is most of your time spent working towards those goals?
- Does this work make you feel accomplished and dignified?
- What tasks or current work is not serving you?
- Do you finish everything you set out to do?
- Are you putting off necessary work? Why?
- What is one thing you remove, add or change in your daily activity that would create momentum in the right direction?

If these questions are difficult to answer it is likely you do not have a clear list of your goals written down somewhere: Here is the best way to remedy that problem:

- Take as much time as you need (hours/days, but no longer) to create a list of clear goals. Make sure to include short and long-term goals in your personal and professional life. Review this list every morning and every evening. It is ok to change or add to this list as you make progress.
- Start planning your days, weeks and months with focused tasks that will help you make progress toward your goals list.
- At day's end, reflect on your progress and evaluate it. Change their priority value if needed.
- Reflect in appreciation on your opportunity to improve, acknowledging what worked and what did not. Be thankful you had the chance to do these things, committing to a new day rooted in that day's activity, not what was done the day before.

When we take life one day at a time, working toward bigger goals and tending to daily needs, we can lay our tired heads down on our pillow at night, sleeping more peacefully because we are dignified in how we spend our time and efforts.

# PERSEVERANCE IS A LIFELONG QUEST

"Many of life's failures are people who did not realize how close they were to success when they gave up."

– THOMAS EDISON

The day came when I realized I was a fraud and a failure! I was a thirty-eight-year-old man with two beautiful boys, along with a big, beautiful, and luxurious home in a nice neighborhood. I was making more money than most physicians with the same practice as me. Life was good from an outsider's perspective, and yet one thing weighed on my mind—my unhealthy relationship with my sons' mother.

Our relationship had deteriorated to the point that we couldn't be our best for these two amazing kids, who were four and two at the time. The problem was that we had different views on what was best for our children. As much as not being with my boys everyday would crush me emotionally, living together had become too much of a strain and I wanted her out of my home. She wanted to stay and pretend that we were a unified family. At the time, I believed this was simply her way of punishing me mentally for failing as a partner. The failure to keep my family together for my kids was psychologically crushing, and the process of separation felt horrific.

I tolerated that living situation for far too long, and one day, just 2 weeks before Christmas, I demanded she move out by month's end. She quickly hired a lawyer and served me with a lawsuit for a ridiculous amount of financial support. That wasn't the worst of it though. The worst was her wanting to limit my access to my sons. This couldn't have come at a worse time.It coincided with mounting pressures at work and a sense of being lost spiritually. For the first time in my life, I was in a state of panic and worry. Why should I work so much at the cost of time with my children only to hand over a large part of those earnings to this woman who obviously didn't care about me.

The toll the drastic change and emotional turmoil those fearful thoughts took on me was extensive and left me exhausted. My sons were my main purpose for my day, every day, and the thought of not having them destroyed my motivation for anything I did. My world was shaken, and I felt shattered.

I let myself carry on in this state of pity for some time. It took the support of my family, friends, and a lot of self-reflection to pull my way out of the hole that I had dug for myself. I had to realize and then accept responsibility for my situation. Luckily taking responsibility also had a huge advantage, because owning my faults meant I could be responsible for the solution. Every single day I worked on becoming a better version of myself. I don't remember how long it took, but one glorious morning I woke up and felt enlightened and reinvigorated. I was a new person with more compassion and understanding. I had no doubt that I was on the right path and that everything would work out in time. I have no idea why or where it came from at that time, but without a doubt, there was zero desire to give up on being my best for my sons. I found myself with rekindled enthusiasm about all things that mattered to me. Recognizing that I had to persevere through a tough situation became important, and it gave me the fight I needed to make it through some of the lowest days I had ever experienced.

I share this event because it has led me to where I am today. This experience helped me realize that everything I experienced in life, good and bad, was a by-product of my beliefs and choices. If I wanted to change my circumstances, I needed to keep pushing my limits. I needed to create a belief system that allowed me to persevere and continue making progress every single day no matter what. This is the belief system that had gotten me from a lowly farm boy to an educated professional dedicated to serving the better good. The best part of this experience was rediscovering that I didn't need anything outside of myself to persevere and get back on my path!

**It was my thirst and curiosity about the world that had gotten me to where I was, and it was only those qualities that would help me to continue growing, learning, and exploring.**

Now I continued working to provide for my sons and with a new purpose in my efforts to learn and help others. They needed me to improve their quality of life and offer stability. Loving them came easy but the steps I needed to take to remain a constant in their life presented challenges at various times. The biggest adjustment I had to make was to my practice and it was immensely stressful. Having the resolve to do what I considered right and my belief system helped me persevere. I started by changing the one thing I had complete control of work! I stopped being an accomplice in a medical system rooted in keeping people sick and dove into leveraging my experience to help all my clients avoid chronic illnesses. Suddenly, I looked forward to every day of work. This newfound energy changed my perspective of everything in my life. My rediscovered commitment to focusing on positivity led to one of life's greatest rewards. As we discussed in Principle 2: Demonstrate Discipline, how you are in one aspect of your life translates to all aspects of your life, my positivity overflowed to my relationship with the mother of my sons. Slowly, as our communication improved, she started to give me more access to my kids!

Why did all this happen? Because I made it through the rough patches and continued on. With every step I took, I became more in tune with my spiritual and moral needs. The process took years, but all the work and effort came together in what felt like an epic "Bam!" moment. After all my suffering, it became clear the changes that seemed sacrificial had made my life better. My practice evolved, putting me in the role of a health guide for my patients instead of a dictator and prescriber of pharmaceuticals. This felt more like what I envisioned a doctor should be: a mentor leading his clients on a path to a place where chronic disease and a life complicated by its consequences are completely avoidable. The dignity in my work brought me a peace that translated to every aspect of my life.

> "Perseverance is not a long race; it is many
> short races one after another."
>
> – WALTER ELLIOT

Since I am human, I still have days that are speckled with doubt. There are still days I seriously consider returning to what I know to be safe. Every day brings on a new challenge to my resolve. I must remind myself every morning of my purpose and reconfirm that I am on the right path. The values I choose to honor are aligned with the beliefs which shape my choices. This approach to everyday challenges incrementally improves my quality of life with every step I take.

**Perseverance doesn't make the process of discovery easier, yet it remains necessary to make the journey.**

You should not forget that to live a life you're proud of requires you to meet challenges head-on. A failed long-term relationship, not capitalizing on a big opportunity, or the death of a loved one are all challenges that bring up regret and can make us waver. Not all days are easy, nor will you successfully persevere every day, and that's okay. The important thing is that you give yourself permission to falter briefly and then quickly get back on track. Perseverance becomes easier when you remind yourself that you are valuable and your contribution to this world makes a difference. The confidence to persevere stems from knowing that you are a trustworthy, honest, empathetic, and determined individual who fights through life's challenges no matter what.

## REFLECTIVE EXERCISE

There are four simple things you can work on right now to tap into this type of perseverance when you feel that you're too tired to go on or are starting to question if what you are pursuing—even if it is your truth—is worth it.

1.  Find a goal worth dying for.
2.  Decide what you want your legacy to be. This may align with what kind of life you would have to lead to become that ideal self.

Decide which philosophy you need to adopt to be your ideal self. Allow yourself to exhibit the traits that would resonate with that ideal.

If these questions are presenting a great difficulty, consider the questions below:

- Are you on a path of your choosing? You must acknowledge the dreams you may have surrendered because they didn't seem realistic, or you didn't want to disappoint your loved ones.
- What would happen if you changed course and decided to pursue your dreams?
- What could you incorporate into your days that would excite you and bring you closer to realizing your dream?
- What is the worst that could happen if you failed to achieve your dream? This is very important, because you will find that fear isn't as bad once you say it out loud and understand you can deal with it and continue to move forward with your life.

No matter what you think, feel, or say to yourself, you cannot escape looking into the mirror and knowing the truth. Honesty is necessary in these moments because it is the only way to ignite your commitment. You will feel liberated when you see yourself overcoming all the obstacles you saw as insurmountable and that your resolve is only getting stronger.

---

# UNDERSTAND YOUR PROGRAMMING

"Too often we confuse 'discovering who we are' with 'discovering who we want to be.' And if we commit to the former it will take care of the latter."

– CRAIG D. LOUNSBROUGH

Did my programming keep me a chubby kid into my late teens? From my earliest memories my mother's words were ones of love and reassurance. Multiple times a day, every day, my mother would tell me how beautiful, smart and perfect I was. Of course, I believed it! Why wouldn't I? My mother knew me better than anyone so how could she be mistaken? It was that same love that led her to spoil me in the only way she could, with food! When I was a child, my family was very poor, but we always had an abundance of food. Like most traditional Mexican families, love is demonstrated with food. Keeping the men and boys well fed is a point of pride for a woman of this culture. That, coupled with my mother's immense love and acceptance, enabled my overeating. When I look back at pictures of me as a kid, I recall how I believed that I was perfect! My mother had convinced me through very deliberate and persistent conditioning that I was everything she believed me to be.

It wasn't until I was about 13 years old that I noticed I was not what I wanted to be physically. That was when I started competing athletically with other kids. I remember the first time I got to compete in the shotput in a state-wide track and field meet and other boys my age were lean and muscular. For the first time in my life, I could see I was a chubby kid! The other kids were stronger and more effective in competition than I was. This sparked an obsession with fitness that changed how I saw myself. I came home from that meet and began to research how to become a better athlete. I learned about weight training and the importance of nutrition. NOT eating but using food as fuel to optimize nutrition. I became increasingly aware of who I wanted to be and how who I was then did not resemble that ideal even remotely.

My mother had some issues with these changes. She insisted on her daily reassurance and programming. Although I had become aware of her influence, I couldn't blame her. Turns out most mothers see their kids as perfect regardless of their obvious imperfections. We argued this point a lot until one day the funniest thing happened.

The Junior High School I attended was hosting "a dance." My best friend and I were able to get dates and our parents bought us nice fancy dress-up clothes, which we never had a use for until then. Our parents came together for the experience and see us off to the dance. My friend, who shall remain nameless, is one of the nicest people I've ever known and a phenomenal athlete. He was not, however, good-looking. His mother, upon seeing him dressed up and ready to head off to "the dance" said, "My son is so handsome! No wonder the girls just cannot help themselves." She continues to caress him and tell him out loud how smart, beautiful, and perfect he was. My mom and I looked at one another and smiled. To this day we both recall this story and laugh because she saw that her perception of me was biased. Although not intentional and purely out of love, she contributed to a complacency in me that I was no longer comfortable with. From that day forward she supported my efforts to change one hundred percent, but continued to insist that, in her eyes, I was and always will be perfect.

> Sometimes the programming is not intentional, but it can be just as impactful as intentional programming. It's interesting to me that most programming is not verbal. Observing behaviors and patterns in daily life leads to subconscious formulations of personality traits and life-shaping habits.

In my parents' home, the roles were clear. My father was and is the quiet hard-working provider that outsiders viewed as strict, stern, and sometimes even controlling. In reality, he is a kind, gentle and loving man that allows his wife to direct the household. "Happy wife, happy life," seems to be his philosophy. I saw how my father accepted his role and lived every day with joy. Despite struggling financially and likely emotionally, as his son I would never have known because he displayed nothing but stoicism and pride in his role. If he had ever experienced existential doubt, I would never know because he never voiced it and exuded a strong sense of contentment. I believe this example is why most boys follow in the footsteps of their fathers. This is the ideal of how a man should be and what he should strive to achieve. To this point, many boys I grew up with ended up staying in their hometown and working the same or similar jobs as their fathers. Therefore, the risk of me ending up an agricultural worker was high.

How did I avoid that fate? PROGRAMMING! My mother told me every day since before I could speak that I would NOT conform to my family's standards. Through daily mantras and persistent messaging, my brain was wired to think much larger than my eyes could see. I wanted to rise above what I saw around me and that meant I had to extract the beneficial parts of what I saw others doing, such as their work ethic and integrity, and use it for my own life.

My specific ethnic and cultural upbringing came with certain programming and assumed stereotypes. Even now, there are times that people are surprised I speak English without an accent. I cannot count how many times I was written off due to assumptions that, like most immigrant children, I was missing a lot of schooling and lacking knowledge. There are still times that people are surprised by my education and accomplishments after learning of my background. I have had to learn to not get angry or even frustrated. Instead, I make it my pleasure to speak up and show the world that I have a voice that is clear, educated and respectfully opinionated. There is great joy in changing people's opinions about "my people" and our capacity to thrive as productive members of society.

This doesn't mean that there is never doubt. I would be lying if I told you that there aren't times when I question whether my reality is just a dream. I have had thoughts that someone will figure it all out someday and send me back to the farm I came from (which wouldn't be all that bad since I loved it there). Thankfully, I am able to shut out those little voices of doubt and remind myself of the strength within, rooted exactly in the background and upbringing in question.

Interestingly, although my parents raised me to be different, there was still some cultural programming my parents couldn't look past. A specific example of this is the programmed notion that you cannot question people of authority or that have some influence over your life and decisions. My parents were frequently embarrassed as I spoke up to defend them or other community members who couldn't do so themselves.

In the tiny community I grew up in, few adults and no children spoke English. Because I was the only person that spoke both English and Spanish well enough to translate, by age seven I became the interpreter for the adults in our community. Imagine a child negotiating housing, pay, and time off with the landlord and employer of all the adults in my neighborhood! I have an unforgettable memory of my outspokenness serving the greater good. One gentleman received notice that his mother was very ill and could possibly pass on soon back in Mexico. The problem was that we were in the middle of harvest season at the farm, and he was afraid to lose his job and housing if he was to leave. I took initiative and went to the boss myself, explained the situation, and negotiated paid leave for this man in addition to better housing arrangements for his family. "Ask and you shall receive," says the bible. Very different from the "keep your head down, quiet and just work" programming we were culturally raised on.

## REFLECTIVE EXERCISE

When we want to understand our programming better, it is up to us to rely on our gut instincts more than that doddering voice in our minds.

In my life, I have found that my intuition is in my gut. It is there that I first process every event or situation. The brain eventually gratefully acknowledges or detrimentally ignores my gut instinct, but usually my instinct is correct. You may be different, and your intuition may be in your heart or your mind. Either way, it is important to identify this intuition and listen closely. When I come across situations or decision paths here is how I process them:

- Is this the right decision for me? Meaning, is this aligned with my goals?
- How will this decision impact those close to me and am I ok with that?
- What does my gut tell me if I make the opposite decision?
- Is that uncomfortable feeling my instincts or is it my programming fighting my instincts?

When something doesn't feel right, that is a solid indicator that it is not right. This is when it becomes necessary to look past programmed responses and listen to your instinct! Be wary of the ego as it is programmed to protect you from feeling anything uncomfortable, even if it is the best path forward.

\* \* \*

By gaining an understanding of why we respond in the ways that we do, we gain the knowledge to take steps to rely on our intuition over our programmed responses. Doing this is a step that will lead to a stronger connection with your authentic self.

# GOOD THINGS UNFOLD NATURALLY WHEN YOU ARE IN ALIGNMENT

"Growth is never by mere chance; it is the result of forces working together."

– JAMES CASH PENNEY

Have you ever found yourself working so much and so hard that you can't find time to step back and appreciate your accomplishments? That was exactly my situation from 2013 to 2014. Every day of the week I was rounding on patients at three different hospitals and as many nursing homes in San Diego County as humanly possible. I couldn't even estimate the number of patients I saw every single day, but it should have been illegal! I was working 24/7 and most days blended together. I was went through each day in a zombie-like fugue; that's how insane the work schedule was.

Around the same time, Medicare (the government funded health insurance which most of my patients were covered by) announced that there were going to be penalties for not providing good care in the hospital. So, if you had patients that were coming back to the hospital for the same reason as previous visits, us doctors were going to be penalized financially. How fair is that? We doctors are already overworked, underpaid and, worst of all, underappreciated.

I looked at this new policy and felt alarmed. How could I be held responsible for patients that were no longer in my care? Once they left my care in the hospital or nursing home they were being cared for by a different doctor. The patients were responsible for getting their own medicines from the pharmacy and making sure they were compliant was impossible! This gap in the continuum of care was problematic, not only for patients who were already confused enough, but for the doctors like me who just couldn't fill all the gaps in this healthcare system. It was this problem that inspired a brilliant idea! Wouldn't it be great if we had the same group of doctors following patients across the spectrum of care? It was crazy to even fathom an idea like this. How amazing would it be to create a system in which all doctors communicated directly and clearly with other doctors and their patients. This would surely eliminate all the miscommunications that lead to a significant number of patients bouncing in and out of the hospital unnecessarily.

**Alignment with yourself is hard enough.
Aligning with others isn't any easier.**

Although I sensed I was on to something, it wasn't well received by my colleagues. They had their own programming (like we discussed in Principle #6), and although most agreed with my perspective, they could not conceive the concept of changing the traditional ways of the doctor's practice. My gut told me I was onto something great! I couldn't let it go and I insisted to my colleagues. Not long after, I was able to secure a contract with a local managed care company to implement my idea. With a contract in hand, I was able to recruit about fifty physicians (every single one skeptical but happy about the pay structure) and forty nurse practitioners to my team. As a team, we covered the full spectrum of care delivery, and we were able to provide better health outcomes for our patients. Ultimately, we were preventing unnecessary hospitalizations which meant better quality of life for our patients and less health care costs for the managed care organization! I felt so empowered being able to build such a company with an extraordinarily diverse team. With great power comes great responsibility however, and I found myself working more than ever!

I was working far too much, but everything seemed to be going well until I was informed that our contract was not being honored and we were no longer getting paid for our efforts. Despite clear evidence that our systems and care delivery were saving millions of dollars and delivering better care to our patients, the managed care company we had partnered with refused to pay us for our services. After two years of funding the project personally, my company was bankrupt. I had no choice but to shut down operations. This failure left me devastated and confused. How did I fail? Where did I go wrong? Was it really me or did I trust the wrong people? The answer became painfully clear and personally devastating. I was so caught up in executing my plans and ideas that I lost track of the most important factor that had landed me the opportunity in the first place.

I'd failed miserably, and that came with a lot of financial backlash for me. Not to mention the emotional and psychological shift I had to endure. I thought I was aligned with the right mission and all metrics pointed to success, but I had failed to maintain the relationship the secured me the contract in the first place. The opportunity came because I had a close and personal relationship with the leaders of the managed care company. They believed in me and believed we were aligned in our goals. As I became overwhelmed with work, I became less present in that relationship. My absence and disconnection lead to doubt in our alignment. Lack in alignment meant NO TRUST! No trust meant the relationship was over!

It was not until writing this book and processing the events of this time that I was able to see my responsibility in this failure. I can tell you with confidence that the reason I failed was my lack of alignment. When I started that project, my motivation was to capitalize financially from their need, and I was simply in the right place to recognize it. I also had a huge debt burden from medical school, a mortgage, car payments, and, of course, supporting my family. I had lost my sense of self and forgotten that what I really cared about and what drove me was helping people live their best lives. I had forgotten that only when I act out of love alone and am aligned morally, spiritually, and emotionally is success guaranteed.

Today, my work isn't guided by its financial output. It's based on service to those who deserve and need my attention. I love what I do and the people I work with. Most days I cannot even call what I do work.

**I have finally gotten myself aligned spiritually, emotionally, mentally, and physically, and it has made a significant difference in all aspects of my personal and professional life.**

When you love what you do, everything naturally unfolds so you can focus on the joy of service. Financial returns become a consequence of your value and the service you provide. ever since my focus changed to the joy of serving others, people and projects deserving of my attention seem to find me with ease. I may not generate as much money as I once did, but what I do get I value so much more because it does not require sacrificing myself to earn it. Being aligned makes it easy to know when to trust the right people with the right intentions. All of this adds up to an extraordinary satisfaction with my work and makes demonstrating discipline, perseverance, and dignity in every project I am involved with a natural outcome.

I feel so fortunate to have arrived at this place of freedom. My freedom is now based on a clear mind, a true sense of accomplishment, peace in all aspects of my life, and most importantly, the flexibility to be present in every moment of my days. Since finding alignment beliefs, decisions and direction seem to fall into place. Long gone are the days when worry about paying bills and finding time for a nap consumed me. True alignment allows me to find meaning in all experiences which directly translates to happiness.

## REFLECTIVE EXERCISE

The process of alignment is not a new concept to most people. That doesn't mean that it is easy to understand. There are multiple forces working together to create opportunities that you must embrace. There are beliefs that you must let go of before progress can be made.

If you wonder if you're on the right path, and you are tremendously uncomfortable, then likely you are on the right path. Challenging every belief and questioning all of your programming is the only way to find alignment. Remember, it is a bumpy path because nobody gets it perfect. It's the challenges along the path that lead to growth towards alignment. The path is bumpy, but the journey is magical and rewarding. Everything feels right in the most incredible ways when you are in alignment with your purpose.

I have found these steps to be valuable in reaching my place of alignment because they allowed me to better understand my authentic motives, desires, and behaviors. It's a combination of all these components, really. Ponder these questions:

- What are my morals?
- How do you feel about yourself on a spiritual level?
- How about on a physical level?
- How do you feel about who you are as a son/daughter, husband/wife, dad/mom, friend/lover? Are you the same person in every role? If not, why not?

You can't be at your best emotionally if you're not aligned. By denying this, you invite struggles into your life. You start seeing that aspects of your life aren't going well. One area of your life may be fine, but another area could be falling apart at the same time because you are not fully aligned. You cannot have certain traits and actions in one area of your life and not practice them in another—that just does not work.

Now, look at how you care for yourself.

- Are you kind or too hard on yourself?
- How do you personally contribute to those beliefs and habits that do not work in your favor?
- What are your views on revealing vulnerability? (Vulnerability can show great strength of character.)

In order to work toward alignment, take these steps to recognize your starting point.

Write down:

- The aspects of life that are important to you and going well (fatherhood, for example)
- The aspects of life that are not going well (challenging children, for example)
- The elements of your work that you enjoy (meeting new people, for example)
- The elements of work that you do not enjoy (billing, for example)

Use the joy of what is going well personally and professionally as a catalyst to start resolving that which is not going well for you. Work on challenging yourself to let go of beliefs and traits that don't work. Then work on applying the beliefs and traits that do work in one aspect of your life to the aspect of your life you are struggling with.

\* \* \*

In the complex symphony of life, alignment brings an invigorating simplicity. You learn to accept that strategies either work or do not work as you intend them to. Knowing the difference and having control of your response to them changes your life. It's important to keep in mind that you cannot control what others say and do, or what happens around you, but the one thing you can control is how you interpret those things and your response.

# SUCCESS ISN'T A TITLE; IT'S LIVING YOUR CALLING

"Success isn't about the end
result, it's about what you
learn along the way."

– VERA WANG

I felt like a phony! In my heart, all the material possessions I had acquired were daily reminders of the exact things that made me insecure. If success is "the progressive realization of an ideal goal," then there was no way I was successful. In fact, it had been so long since I felt like a success that I couldn't even remember when I deviated from my path. All I had was a pervasive feeling that I despised the person I had allowed myself to become. I had to figure out how to regain my bearings and get back on my path as soon as possible. I had been working for 15 years since finishing my medical training and felt further away from my ideal goal than ever. The insurmountable challenge suddenly became: "How do I even begin changing my reality? What is the root cause of my problem?" The redirection and personal evolution necessary to transition from what I had become to a man walking steadily on the path toward success was neither easy nor seamless. It didn't take days; it took years. The biggest breakthrough came when I realized that being honest with myself and living my truth every single day emotionally freed me. This newly discovered emotional freedom led to a newfound love and appreciation of myself. That self-love translated directly to love for all others and appreciation of every opportunity to improve. As you can likely imagine, living in appreciation generated an abundance of positive energy that I passed on to everyone and everything in my life.

**"You must become what you want to attract."**

– MARSHALL SYLVER

I was now vibrating at a much higher frequency which attracted others on the same level. This became clear to me when, out of the blue, I received a message from a lady who had worked in my area, but had never crossed paths with me. She wrote in her message that my name and my approach to medicine had come up in conversations with colleagues, and she was interested in meeting to possibly work together on her new project! As it turns out, she had a desire to bring precision medicine to the masses. Her goal was to make precision medicine affordable and accessible to everyone by leveraging telemedicine technology. This resonated with me because I would be able to serve rural communities like the one I grew up in. More importantly, I would be providing precision care for families that are less socioeconomically privileged. This aligned perfectly with my morals and goals!

> **It almost feels like opportunities fall from the sky when you are aligned.**

The company was in its infancy, but I excitedly joined the startup at the ground level. I quickly found myself working with educated, dedicated, and energizing individuals all committed to a single purpose. I was involved in creating something that would revolutionize the medical world! This was exactly what I needed. I looked forward to my work every day because the people I was collaborating with were experienced, proven leaders in their field, and still demonstrated a great respect for my knowledge, perspectives, and ideas. This is rare in traditional medicine, where physicians are treated more like cheap labor; secretaries who write prescriptions and move people through the system as quickly as possible. I loved this new role so much that I agreed to do it for almost no pay!

> **What you do to prepare for new opportunities day-to-day makes a massive difference in getting you set for your "big moments."**

I am sure you are familiar with the cliché "It is better to be ready and not needed than be needed and not ready." This is not as easy as it sounds. Making strides towards your best self every day is the ideal goal, but to keep making those strides when you aren't sure what you're preparing for makes the daily process difficult. Some days it may be learning new skills or adding knowledge that makes you more valuable. Other days, it may be necessary to eliminate thoughts or habits that inhibit your mindset and progress. However, the resolve to whittle away daily at becoming "better," even in small ways, can take you further than you may have ever imagined.

Doubts do exist, challenges arise, and thankfully, solutions present themselves too. The key is staying committed to what you believe in. There should be no amount of financial compensation that can deter you from adhering to your morals, values, and beliefs. No amount of money should lead you away from your path to fulfilment.

By knowing your strengths, challenges, and the tools you have available, you can make positive strides every day or, at least, not move backwards. If you happen to move in the wrong direction one day, you learn from your mistakeand redirect the next day to try again.

**Connecting with what you are designed to do in life breathes this fantastic energy into you. You notice your transformation, and it becomes exhilarating.**

Working with people I was morally and ethically aligned with compelled me to become better every day. The work we were doing didn't feel like "work" at all. It was joyful and exciting to make strides towards bringing it to fruition. It felt like I was hanging out with my three best friends every day, and it was delightfully productive despite not having all that much money. I was so inspired by all of this that I'd even go to bed and dream about what I was doing. This positivity also helped me refocus on my health and personal relationships. I found that during this time I became so aligned that making the right choices in all aspects of my life came effortlessly.

> "You can't get from point A to point B if
> you aren't already at point A."
>
> – JORDAN PETERSON

For you, finding success can feel the same way. It starts by understanding where precisely you are now (point A) and then determining where precisely you want to be (point B). This also requires you to analyze how you feel about your current position; is it exciting or aggravating? Do you look forward to your work, or do you dread it? Are you trying to fit a mold that you are not designed to be in (called impostor syndrome)? Knowing these answers is important, and the only path forward is by being 100 percent honest with yourself.

There is no shame in any answer. You must know that you're not pinpointing exactly where you are in life to shame yourself, but instead allow yourself to set one foot firmly in the known. With one foot on solid ground, it becomes much easier to step with the other foot into the unknown, taking comfort in the knowledge that you are making progress towards your ideal goal. Those steps, that journey, and the joy that progress provides are the definition of success!

## REFLECTIVE EXERCISE

It's time to learn what you can start doing to live your calling, which is one of the most exciting steps you can take. Seriously, even the worst day becomes better than your previous best day when you are aligned and making progress.

1.  Start by identifying exactly where you are in your life: professionally, personally, and spiritually.
2.  How do you feel about where you are now?
    *   Acknowledge and accept what creates anxiety/discomfort. Use this anxiety/discomfort to motivate change.
    *   Now turn your thoughts to those that evoke positive responses.
3.  Think of what you have wanted to do that has been put on the back burner. Are those things still of interest to you? Is this your ideal goal?
    *   What would be the first step in this direction? Maybe you don't start with a step, but instead just turn your attention to the path.
    *   Set a timeline for when you will take the first step and make an accountability plan.

As you keep taking these steps from point A to point B you will find yourself more in alignment with your calling, and, in time, feeling successful.

Important to notice: As you set a path toward your ideal goal, make sure it is *your* ideal, not someone else's expectation of you. It is ok to continue to alter your path as you make progress. The more steps you take into the unknown, the more you will get to know yourself. That self-knowledge and self-awareness may lead to a new and evolved ideal. No one else can show you the right path. It is that portion of uncertainty that creates excitement and makes life worthwhile. Success is only measured by progress down the path of your choosing!

# FIND YOUR COMMUNITY

"We cannot live only for ourselves.
A thousand fibers connect
us with our fellow men."

– HERMAN MELVILLE

My fortune has come from finding myself surrounded by extraordinary people everywhere I go! I describe my community as the network of people I interact with or those who are somehow involved with my life. Whether they are at the grocery store, work, or the coffee shop, good people radiate positivity, and I am instantly attracted. I have been fortunate to find amazing people everywhere I've lived. When it was time to move on, it was the people that made it an emotional goodbye. Incredibly, every new environment has led me to new people and new opportunities for impact and growth. I know you are thinking that my outlook sounds far too positive, and I have, at times, encountered less desirable members of a community. I have been burnt and disappointed, but what I couldn't do was allow those few bad people to change my outlook on the community at large. I chose to bring positivity and let that flow through my surroundings.

When I was growing up, my community was small—all the people in those seven dollars a week homes on the farm. Almost everyone was related to me in some way, and that meant there was a lot of love. It was a humble, caring environment that I enjoyed being immersed in. However, there was also a lot to learn about the world that existed outside this community, and that was both important to me and shocking at first.

When we moved into town and away from the tight-knit community on the farm, everything was so different. We had new neighbors who didn't work on the farms, and the stores and shops around us were not what we were used to. To top it off, the types of people we interacted with were completely different because they were typically more educated, wealthier, and held a different worldview.

How was I ever going to figure it all out? As a 9-year-old kid, these thoughts were daunting.

This new world I had transitioned into changed my outlook. Exposure to my new community helped me understand why a good education mattered. The messaging I received from this new community was evidence that my mother's strong belief in education was justified. My intent, when my family moved from the farm, was to hold on to my relationships and beliefs because I felt safe there, but suddenly I realized that the old philosophy would no longer serve me well. It didn't take long before I found myself surrounded by an extraordinary new community that elevated me in every aspect of my life.

**As my community changed, and it has several times, there is always a fundamental core group of people who seemed to connect with me and, most importantly, care.**

From the little farm town I grew up in, to college at UC Davis, to medical school in Los Angeles, to my residency training at UC San Diego Medical Center, and thereafter in "the real world," my communities have changed but their contribution to my life has not. From each of these I found at least one person that I bonded with deeply, and those friends are their own community I take with me everywhere I go. Each community provided someone that challenged me personally, another that helped me improve physically, and yet another that encouraged me to grow spiritually. The qualities that each community of people provided for me were the same ones I offered them. It became clear to me that in life we get what we give! Each community propelled me to continue my growth journey and expand my wings. They each embedded themselves deeply in my life while we were together, but also encouraged me to move on when I had outgrown that community. As much as we meant to one another, they made me feel comfortable moving onward to share my gifts. The strength I drew from each community I have been a part of has been essential in my ability to keep reaching and taking steps into the unknown.

"Alone we can do so little; together we can do so much."

– HELEN KELLER

It took a village to survive in some of these communities, especially when I was young. Living in a small farm town with little resources meant we relied on each other for a lot. My parents perhaps offered someone vegetables in exchange for fruit. Sometimes the help requests demanded more of a commitment, but there was always someone in our community who would step up. These exchanges helped us all be better off and satisfy our basic needs enough that I didn't realize how poor we were. I experienced firsthand why, at times, being part of a unified community is necessary. Every single person in a community, especially small rural ones, serves a role and has a purpose.

Community, in current times, has taken on an expanded definition. With extraordinary connectivity in the world, we now influence and are influenced by people who may live on a different continent. This doesn't mean that our contribution and what we take away from our community is any different. This is a lesson that has been difficult to impress upon my sons. Their community includes a great many people: parents, educators, family, friends, and certainly all the people they interact with daily via the internet on their video games and social media platforms. I would argue that those latter groups have more influence than the people they interact with in person. The difficulty lies in learning how to extract the positive and release the negativity that we are exposed to. My philosophy remains the same: In life, you get what you give! I encourage them to exude positivity and always act out of love.

**"The greatness of a community is most accurately measured by the compassionate actions of its members."**

– CORETTA SCOTT KING

I want to impress this upon you the same way I hope to demonstrate this to my sons. The only way to grow and make sure that you are contributing positively to your community—or even strangers—is by sharing your gifts. This became obvious during the COVID-19 pandemic. My sons, like most kids in our world, became disconnected from their classmates and teachers. They were forced into a "distance learning" program that meant classes were broadcast via Zoom. Each of my sons would wake up just seconds before they had to log into their zoom for class, while still in bed, and often still sleeping, they would get through their entire day of classes. It didn't take long to see that they were learning nothing in this manner. More tragically, there was no connection with their teachers or classmates.

This could NOT go on! We sat together to discuss a solution. They argued that the curriculum was boring in person and virtually it was near impossible to engage. I encouraged them to speak up and inform their teachers that this method of learning was just not cutting it and if they wanted to engage their students, a more stimulating and involved lesson plan would be necessary. Their teachers were also disengaged and couldn't think past their own survival through this challenging time. After much deliberation, we had an extraordinary breakthrough! What if each class started with 5-10 min of social engagement time? This would certainly allow the children to reconnect with their friends and teachers, wake them up, and hopefully feel more involved in the lesson for the day. I challenged my boys to then use their positive energy to help their classmates and teachers feel better about themselves even under the stressful circumstances. To this day

I am unsure if we made a difference in the curriculum or their ability to learn, but I do know we helped bring their community closer and all their classmates become more engaged as humans sharing similar difficulties.

**It is better to outgrow a community and move past it than to limit your potential and hold on for dear life.**

I love pizza! More specifically, Village Host Pizza in the town I grew up in. It still makes my mouth water just thinking about that deliciously soft dough, cheesy crust, and plentiful toppings! In high school, one of my good friends worked as a delivery boy for Village Host Pizza, and we took advantage of his position by getting discounted or free pizzas on a regular basis. I have such nostalgia and love for that pizza that I frequently order pizza from there when I visit my parents. Not long ago, on one of my pizza runs, I was waiting at the bar for my pizza to finish baking when my buddy who delivered pizzas for them in high school runs up to the counter. I had not seen him in 25 years, so we hugged with excitement and chatted a bit. He shared that he was still living in the same home with his parents, and he was delivering pizzas for Village Host in addition to driving for Uber. He quickly asked where I was living and what I was doing with my life. As soon as I shared what I had accomplished professionally and personally since high school he quickly became uncomfortable and abruptly ended our conversation. It would have been great to chat a bit longer as we had shared a lot of good times together in high school, but now there was a huge wedge between us that he couldn't see past. It was not my intention to make him feel lesser, and in no way does my education or accomplishments make me feel superior to anyone. My friend had the same potential and community support that I did. He chose not to live up to that potential. Was it due to fear of outgrowing such a wonderful community and holding on to that life we loved so much? I will never know. He may not know. What I do know is the only way forward is to be proud of yourself, treat everyone with respect, and accept that everyone in your community has an impact on your life directly or indirectly. I know that by striving to improve myself, wherever I am, I will be contributing to my community. If you do the same, your community will offer more than money in return.

## REFLECTIVE EXERCISE

A lot of people struggle to understand their community: who does it involve, and what importance does it have? Take some time to identify who you see as your community, and list the answers to these questions:

- List all the members of your community.
- How do each of these members contribute to your life?
- What are your positive contributions to your community?
- What positives does your community provide you?
- Have you outgrown your community?
- What other communities are a part of your life? (Examples are church, school, sports league, etc.)
- Could you be more involved in those communities?
- Are you sharing the best of you with your community?
- Everyone has a unique role and gift to offer a community. Your community needs you more than ever now. You also need that support to live up to your own potential. It can be as easy as volunteering, coaching or just helping clean here and there. Don't underestimate the contributions you can make. Think about the ways that you view community in your life. Find the connectors that allow you to integrate. Get to know others and make yourself known in turn.

\* \* \*

The essence within all of us begins to reveal itself to our first community, which is our family. As we grow older, we become a part of this community for someone else, and with that comes the great responsibility of ensuring we use our gifts within our given community for good.

# EMBRACE EFFECTIVE SUPPORT NETWORKS

"Inspiration, from whatever the source, arouses feelings within us that rekindle hope, ambition, and determination. It is a momentary whisper of encouragement and reassurance that causes us to become aware of our potential."

– JIM ROHN

If you're uncertain about what an effective support network is, there is a good chance you don't have one. Unlike community, a support network likely includes a variety of people from various walks of life and locations.

Once you've identified the type of person you are and accept who you are, you can benefit greatly from having an effective support network. These are the people who hold you accountable to being your best, offer insights and strategies on managing your weaknesses, and help you find methods to overcome your deficiencies. Examples of sources to find effective support networks are meditation groups, an individual coach such as a life coach, or any individual or group that helps you focus on improvement.

Once you've identified what your needs for a support system are, you can go out and find it, knowing that the people closest to you are likely not the answer. Wait…how could these people not be the answer! If you wondered that, consider that you may have outgrown them, that they are too compassionate to be forthright with you about your challenges, and that it is invigorating to get fresh opinions from people who are not attached to you or the outcome—just the logic of the process.

**Effective support networks take you out of the comfort zone and into the evaluation zone. There is no better way to evolve personally and professionally.**

I know I went through this when I first entered medicine. I was so excited to share my experiences in the medical world with everyone who wanted to be a part of it. Reaching the most people I could was so important to me. To do this, I even tried to create a YouTube channel. I made full scripts and talked about different topics, eager to tell people what others wouldn't.

There was one thing holding me back, and it was a big deal. I wasn't a great public speaker. At least I thought I wasn't, which essentially made it true. I had trusted that by creating these scripts, I would be a better presenter and overcome the fear. In truth, scripts made me very robotic and ineffective. It was all a bit demoralizing, but it was obviously a problem that I needed to overcome if I was to achieve my goal.

I had no idea what to do at first. So, I went online and looked up public speaking to get some pointers. I ended up finding a public speaking and development coach that I hired. This stretched me to the limits and made me uncomfortable beyond belief! As nervewracking as it was, it also helped me push myself further than I could have on my own. At first, I thought it was going to be easy (that's the optimist in me), but that was simply my ego trying to protect me. My coach helped me look at myself in a completely different light. To ease me into a growth phase she first had me identify where my strengths were and solidified my belief in those strengths. It was then much easier to accept that I had some major weaknesses or deficiencies, but she also made me believe they were not insurmountable. This newfound support taught me to comfortably speak from my heart and off the cuff. With confidence in my abilities, I became a more effective speaker and learned to face weaknesses with certainty that I could overcome them without compromising myself.

Hiring a coach turned out to be an excellent move in more ways than one. I became a better presenter, and I was attracting other strong individuals that only added to my support network. I connected with other people on the journey to become better public speakers for their goals and helped them improve as well. It was amazing to not feel alone on this journey and even better to help lift others up at the same time. It was so liberating to know that:

1.   My faults were not insurmountable.
2.   My support network could see what my blind spots hid.

As a result, I became a better doctor for my client and patients, and a better associate for my business partners. My support network is invaluable and continues to pay dividends.

As of today, I am writing this book, I am a cohost on a radio show and a podcast where we discuss a variety of health-related topics. It is an unscripted show where we focus on helping our audience become better-educated consumers of health care. We highlight the free choice we all have in deciding our own health trajectory and health span. To date, we have successfully recorded over seventy episodes and I look forward to it every week.

I owe a tremendous amount of gratitude to my support group and coach for helping me fulfill my greater vision with public speaking. It has opened doors to educate other physicians—and individuals not in medicine—on topics that are important to my own community and the world in general. Without this support network helping me overcome my fears and deficiencies, I would not be able to share my message with the world.

### Direct unattached feedback, although emotionally difficult, is worth its weight in gold!

If your intention is self-development, and it should be, consider a support network that goes beyond your personal relationships. Those people who know you well and love you will hold back as to not hurt your feelings. Having someone you pay that is not emotionally tied to you, can critically evaluate you, and give you feedback without fear of losing your friendship is invaluable. I can tell you from personal experience that it is much easier to accept criticism from an unbiased person, and grow from it, than it is from those whom you are emotionally close to. Consider these people personal coaches, and we all need one for every aspect of our life in which perpetual growth and development is essential for success.

## REFLECTIVE EXERCISES

This reflective exercise is going to require that you address what your weaknesses are with the humblest self you can muster.

1.  Which areas of your life do you feel, if improved, would greatly impact your quality of life? Or make you even more valuable?
2.  In which scenarios are you the most uncomfortable or feel the most vulnerable?
3.  Which skills would you like to add to your tool belt that would improve you in these areas of difficulty?
4.  Who do you rely on now to help you evaluate and improve on yourself?
5.  In which areas that you have identified would a coach(es) help you make vast improvement?

I know exactly what you are thinking! "I can't afford coaches!" I was there many times myself, until I learned that coaches saved me so much time in trial-and-error periods. My coaches helped me avoid common pitfalls and accelerated my growth at least tenfold! That kind of time savings is a million times more valuable than the money I spent for their service.

Something to consider during your journey: It is quite possible that at times you will receive more benefit from giving (a.k.a. being the support) than receiving. I have found that by supporting others in their growth I have solidified my own knowledge and better understood where I needed more help.

\* \* \*

Ultimately, support networks are an intricate part of the human experience. It all comes down to acts of love and caring. When you love and care for others, being part of their support network comes naturally and effortlessly. Giving love and support assures you will also experience the same attention in areas where you are lacking. Love and care are the supportive nutrients that help us grow healthier and stronger in our abilities.

# ACCEPTANCE IS ESSENTIAL ON THE PATH TO ALL GROWTH

"You couldn't relive your life, skipping the awful parts, without losing what made it worthwhile. You had to accept it as a whole—like the world, or the person you loved."

– STEWART O'NAN

I couldn't believe it happened, but it did! I allowed my circumstances to change how I saw myself and how I interacted with the world. The change was not sudden, and I am not sure when exactly I started noticing the change, but when I found myself in a world that was punishing, cold and lonely it became obvious I had lost my way. Somewhere along my path, I stopped being true to myself and lost sight of the genuine kindness and empathy for others that had led me to pursue medicine in the first place. Honestly, I found myself feeling a bit lost and aimless for the first time in my life.

This problem of not accepting who I truly was and defining myself as a unique human being is hardly unique to me; most people have had these moments. It became obvious when I started to question even the most mundane occurrences. There was a visceral disdain for just about everything about myself, but it was so general that I couldn't define it properly. This is exactly why I knew the change was slow and insidious in nature: it took many years to notice it! The most obvious change was my lack of identity, which defined my uniqueness that I was raised to be so proud of. I had also lost the joy in my work and in most of the activities which traditionally lit me up. This was not a man I recognized as myself.

**There is great beauty when you accept your life for what it is while also taking steps to grow into someone far greater than you may have ever imagined.**

Willful blindness is the term! Turning a blind eye to things that do not align with you morally because it is easier, and at least in the short term emotionally beneficial to pretend not to notice. Some argue this philosophy is worse than knowingly and willingly contributing to the problem. This was not the kind of person I was raised to be, nor was I proud to have become. In fact, I am still ashamed to admit I allowed myself to develop in that direction. To cope with this challenge, I seemed to have created an altered image of myself—almost like an avatar. This avatar only heard and saw what was necessary to get through my day and continue the farce. You could argue that this sounds like a man that minds his business. That's not so bad, however, this type of philosophy comes with a lofty price. Knowing who you are and not sharing yourself completely not only deprives the world of your gifts, but also limits the experiences the world can offer you! For me, it led to the feeling that I never quite belonged or fit in, and that took its toll on me. The man I was outwardly was quite different from the thoughts that swirled inside me. It was a form of impostor syndrome, and I knew the day would come when everyone would figure it out, and I'd be exposed for the phony I was. Those thoughts consumed my mind, and I lived in fear that I would soon be exposed.

One of my recollections happened on my first day of medical school classes. I met a young lady who sat next to me, a top-tier graduate from Harvard. She had grown up in this elaborate life where she was best friends with Quincy Jones' daughters and socialized with the elite in our society. On the other side of me sat another impressive young man who presented an impressive resume including world travels and whose father was the dean of the medical school at the University of Colorado. My medical school class was full of fantastical people with amazing backgrounds and powerhouse stories. I questioned how and why I had gotten there and worst of all I questioned whether I deserved to be there at all.

It wasn't that I felt ashamed of my background. I just felt like I had nothing to contribute, and that's when I started to think about the one area I could compete in, and that was my work ethic and academics. No one would care about my shortcomings if I was impressing them academically and standing out as a top student in our class.

**Being emotionally closed off and strictly academic-focused is no way to find happiness.**

This strong feeling of insecurity about my opportunity always reminded me that I was in the wrong place—that I didn't belong. Because I didn't believe I belonged others also felt pushed away. I was fortunate to have created a couple of life-long friends in medical school. Those were the two that saw past my insecurities and worked their way into my trust. I am grateful for them to this day. That same gut-wrenching feeling carried on all the way through my residency and as you can imagine it led to a very difficult three years from a political standpoint. It turns out that in these academic settings it benefits you to fit in, play along, and be liked by the leadership staff. It does not matter if you are great academically and your patient care is flawless. To be seen as great you must play the political game and I couldn't do it at that time. I couldn't get past my insecurities and still wasn't allowing my true self to come through. Interestingly, I remember the day I was forced to take a good look at myself and see what I had been avoiding for years.

I had finally finished residency and was going out on my own to start working as a full-fledged doctor. As I was packing to move homes, I found my medical school badge with a picture on it that had been taken during my orientation. I looked so different, aside from how one would change with age. The look in my eyes was different. I took that picture and went to a mirror to compare it to the current version of me. As I did so, memories of who I was flooded back to me. As I took this reflective journey, I began to remember who I used to be and those qualities that made me special— sure of myself, confident, enthusiastic, energetic, excited, and, most of all, proud. That was the genuine me, the real deal, and the person I was born and raised to be.

**When I finally accepted that I didn't have anything to prove to anyone other than myself, I felt so free. A great burden had been lifted, and I could finally grow from what I'd learned.**

Your life doesn't have to be filled with big names to have an interesting story.

It's better to have a humble family filled with love than a family that stays busy to avoid each other.

In general, it is always best to simply and humbly be your best self and work toward worthy outcomes.

When you learn to accept your story and who you are, you will gain strength and know your worth. By doing this exact thing, I could fully be myself and become open and emotionally available. This led to fitting in more and added new dimensions to the growth I was experiencing. To recognize this and act on it was extraordinarily liberating.

What was even better is that those people who were not meant to be in my life moved on, and those who embraced my authenticity have remained friends all these years later. Think about your life and your friends. The genuine friends—not acquaintances—that have lasted a long time know you and your story. You don't have to fake anything with them.

Revealing your vulnerability to others leads to incredible outcomes. For one, you begin to feel more comfortable. You no longer live in fear of people discovering who you really are and then wanting nothing to do with you. If they don't want to be your friend, that's fine. You know you're better off with one authentic friend than five who are not.

Another benefit of accepting who you are is that self-knowledge lessens anxiety. Remember, I am not typically an anxious person, but I had anxiety when I was trying to be a different person than who I was designed to be. This meant that, at times, I couldn't express myself in a way that showed my strengths because I discredited the positive impact my genuine self could have. With acceptance came freedom!

**Not everybody has to like you. If you're true
to yourself, not everyone will.**

Face it; even if you won't admit it, deep down at your core, you know exactly who you are. Embracing that true self is necessary if you are to make any positive contribution to the world. Don't confuse knowing with accepting who you are. I always knew I was the son of Mexican migrant workers, just like I know the sky is blue and the sun will rise every day. However, accepting who I am reminds me that I am ever grateful for my parents and how they've contributed to my life, just as I am appreciative of a sunny day and a beautiful sunrise. Recognizing this is the driving force of acceptance. When you're completely open about who and what you are, others will reveal their own vulnerability as they will trust you innately. This unity with the world opens doors in the most incredible ways allowing you to impact everyone you touch and bringing meaning to everything you do.

You can leave fear and anxiety behind and allow love and caring to be your drive—the qualities that define you can take the helm and guide you to marvelous places.

I am Guillermo Castillo, a uniquely valuable contributor to this world, and I'll never forget it again. Who are you?

## REFLECTIVE EXERCISE

It's time to recognize and accept who you are, and align that person with the world you chose to live in. Start here:

1.  list out all those contributions and characteristics that define you.
    *   Be honest and include the good and not so good. Just acknowledge that they are a part of you.
2.  Next, take that list and share which items you accept entirely.
    *   This is noted by the pride or gratitude they give you. You define these things as strengths.
3.  List the things that were less good, you don't like, or don't feel good about.
    *   Evaluate the reasons why you may feel this way. Ask these questions of yourself:
    *   How can I turn this belief around?
    *   In what ways does this belief hinder me or not help me?
    *   How can I turn a hindering belief into a positive?
    *   Which of these can I throw away?
    *   How can I apply this attribute and make it my own?

* * *

These strategies offer a way to unite the authentic self with the heart and mind, and the resilience to grow in the most amazing ways.

# LET INTEGRITY COURSE THROUGH YOUR VEINS

"With integrity, you have nothing to fear, since you have nothing to hide. With integrity, you will do the right thing, so you will have no guilt.

– ZIG ZIGLAR

When I was a young boy, one of my dad's friends approached him with an opportunity to drive a truck and "make lots of money." Of course, my dad was curious, and since money was always in short supply, that made it worth asking a few more questions. Thank goodness he did because it turns out the job was likely in the realm of transporting illegal substances, and my dad immediately turned his back on the idea. He clearly stated that it went against everything he stood for, and why would he want to bring substances into this country that people might sell to his children? Dad showed a massive amount of integrity in a time when our family needed the money. My dad made it clear that there was no amount of money worth compromising his peace of mind or morals. We later found out that this childhood friend of my dad ended up in prison. As far as I know, my dad never saw him again.

**I'll never forget that story and the lessons it taught me.
Not only was it immoral and wrong, despite the payday,
but doing such a thing would have cost my dad the pride
that allowed him to hold his head high in any room.**

As an adult, I received a challenge to my integrity that forced me to decide what type of man I wanted to be at that moment. I was working at a prominent hospital in San Diego, California. The hospital billed the insurance companies based on my documentation of patient severity in my progress notes. So, if I wrote that a patient came in with shortness of breath, and testing determined she had pneumonia, I would treat her for three days, give her antibiotics, and then she'd go home. However, they always had a checklist with other steps you could take or tests you could perform in addition to optimizing the billing codes. This means the hospital could make more money, even if it didn't change the patient's treatment or outcome. One day, they asked me to revise my notes and include a battery of tests that I hadn't done on a patient so they could optimize their bill.

If my hesitation wasn't enough, I am sure I stared at them long and hard with disbelief and shock before I asked them to repeat and clarify their request. I didn't want to believe what I was hearing but other doctors had shared similar experiences. Until now I thought these stories were exaggerations, but now I was living that story. The billing department was insistent with me, and I delayed and eventually refused. Initially, I was told this wasn't a big deal, and it was simply a semantics game. My gut, on the other hand, was SCREAMING "NO WAY!" How could I jeopardize my integrity to do something I felt was wrong just to help the hospital make more money?

Not long after this, coincidentally, the hospital started to give me a harder time about my practice there as an independent physician. I was forced to meet almost impossible expectations if I was to keep my privileges. I did as much as I could to hold on, but in time, I was pushed out of that hospital. Sadly, even though everyone on staff was well aware of the reasons for my persecution, no one spoke up to challenge the system.

Still, I knew I did the right thing. I was able to demonstrate integrity when it might have been easier to simply go along like most everyone else did. However, that is a slippery slope, and letting a situation slide one time often leads to another and then another. Although no patients were hurt by this practice, it was unethical and would have lingered in my conscience.

Now, I know that there are good doctors who perhaps went along with this practice. I don't mean to slam them and suggest I'm better. The experience opened my eyes to the fact that I was part of a system that was not aligned with me ethically or professionally. I wanted to be proud of my profession and feel good about rendering my best care to every patient I encountered.

**"Integrity is the only path where you will never get lost."**

– MIKE MAPLES JR.

When integrity courses through your veins, every principle that I'm sharing with you will become an easier undertaking—even the ones most challenging for you. When integrity is the only path you follow, there is no compromising your principles no matter the circumstance. Everything is done with a purpose that is fueled by your personal integrity—which in turn creates meaning in all your actions.

You will be tested on your integrity every single day. That is just part of a good life's turbulence. This may be things as simple as getting up every day at 5am to start your day with meditation and a good workout. It could be as difficult as confronting a colleague about their subtle racist or sexist remarks in the workplace that are causing separation amongst the team. Looking the other way will frequently be the easiest choice, but when integrity is second nature your immediate intervention will always produce the right outcomes. Personally, you will also experience an incredible side benefit—honor—and that is a quality to be proud of.

**"Whomever can be trusted with small things can also be trusted with big things."**

– LUKE 16:10

When I was only twelve a new neighbor moved in across the street. It was a family of four. Husband, wife and two identical twins at 3-years-old. The man of the house, Frank was his name, had a garage door repair and replace business, and worked alone. I was a big boy for twelve and in my spare time, Frank would employ me to be his assistant. This meant helping him prepare equipment and anything else he needed an extra hand for. We drove around in his work truck and spent a lot of time together talking and getting to know one another. This means I also had access to all his tools and his family's livelihood. I never missed a day I had committed to working with him and before long he saw I was not only reliable but trustworthy. He and his wife also started to ask me to babysit for his twins so they could go out and spend quality time as a couple. I didn't realize it completely in the moment, but later as an adult I realized that they must have really trusted me completely. They left me in charge of the most valuable gifts in their lives many times: their sons! We became best of friends and remain to this day. I am sure I have thanked him for all his support, but I am not sure I have ever told him how much I appreciate his trust and faith in me. Looking back, once I proved I was a man of integrity at work, he didn't have to question whether I could be trusted with his children.

## REFLECTIVE EXERCISE

Integrity, or its practice, is not always so black and white. I frequently must rely on my gut intuition to help me decide when I am acting out of alignment. This intuitive sense is ever-present and can present daily tests to me, and when a situation doesn't feel right, it is most often because it is not right. It doesn't feel good when you act inappropriately or in a way that doesn't align with your morals and beliefs. These best decisions are not always easy or convenient. And that is okay, sometimes we need to slow our thoughts down to better understand what our actions will truly lead to. It may not always lead you where you thought it would, but when you act with integrity the result will never be one you regret.

Reflecting on integrity is a journey that can leave you feeling uneasy and discontent, depending on how you've used it or ignored it in your life. Today is your fresh start.

1. Begin by listing those situations in your life where something did not go your way. (We all have some of those, don't we?) ~

2. With each of these situations, list what did not go according to your desires and the challenges that arose because of that.
   - Ask yourself why the situation played out in the manner it did, and you'll likely discover it was because you went against a gut instinct that would have kept you aligned with your integrity.

3. Next, list those situations where your decision was based on integrity. What happened in those situations? What felt different to you? What was different about the outcome when your integrity was at work for you?

\* \* \*

Maintaining your integrity will keep you aligned spiritually, emotionally, and psychologically. Finding the way to align with your integrity is a game-changer. It's like the secret ingredient that makes the meal incredible, not simply good. In inexplicable ways, life becomes better when you remember the importance of the honor this brings to your life.

# BE A STUDENT OF LIFE, FOR LIFE

"Curiosity is the wick in
the candle of learning."


– WILLIAM ARTHUR WARD

Being a kid is an awesome time in your life and a time to cherish. Most kids have an innate curiosity about everything. They want to know, explore, and tinker. I remember as a child how fired up I would get for the school day because I knew I would be exploring and learning! My mother played a big role in that excitement because leading up to my first day of school she reminded me frequently how excited she was for me to learn English and then teach it to her. Mom would often say I was the hope for change in our family, and I bought into the notion wholeheartedly.

On that first day of school, I was so excited to return home and share the good news. I ran up to my mom, speaking Spanish, of course, and said, "Mom, Mom, I learned English." She was excited but obviously curious about what I meant, so I shared my one word in English with her.

Now, we all know that hardly means that I really knew English; however, it was the start of a journey, a journey that still carries on today. I may know English well, but I also realize there are endless other things for me to learn.

**I value being a student of life, for life, and that will ensure I continue my path toward success.**

I've always experienced this intense drive to learn and then share my knowledge with the world—or whoever may listen. This carried me from year to year and instilled a desire in me to always be better and do better.

The way I approached education offered a stark contrast to others in my small Hispanic agricultural community. Many of these kids I grew up with merely survived school while growing old enough to help financially support their families. The kids of today will never know the effort it took to gain access to information in the days before the internet. It was the insatiable desire to learn that gave us the energy and drive to hunt down books and periodicals in the library. When I say hunt, it was a true hunt through index cards with reference numbers that correlated with sections, rows, and shelves in the library. The emotional turmoil and defeat when, after so much effort, you arrived at the book's expected location and it was gone! Hopefully, someone else had checked it out and it would eventually find its way back for me. Luckily, I had very supportive parents that drove me to the public library often and encouraged my curiosity.

In this day and age, invaluable information about any topic I desire is at my fingertips! I refuse to go a single day without learning at least one thing that makes me better, even if only in the smallest of ways. Leadership, communication, emotional intelligence, social awareness, and spiritual development have become my favorite learning topics as of late. This type of learning is at the heart of what I do today because it's fun, exciting, and makes me more valuable to everyone I encounter. My joy now comes from helping others optimize their potential and create their self-designed health trajectory. I feel more blessed with every bit of knowledge that develops my own evolution and allows me to share my enthusiasm for life with the world.

**It is wonderful to know that I can unwrap the world layer by layer and learn more about any part of it I desire to know more about.**

This pursuit includes personal items of interest as well as academic rigor. For example, during the writing of this book, I completed a mini-MBA program in rural medicine. I also applied to law school in the hope that I might be able to have an impact on tort reform for medical doctors-one of the many problem areas in our current medical system.

Writing a book is another example. This journey has been an incredible one filled with self-reflection and discovery. I wasn't sure if I'd be able to do this successfully and now, I've been able to prove to myself that I could. It feels amazing, but not as amazing as thinking of this book's potential to help other people elevate their lives in some manner. Whether it is spiritually, academically, emotionally, or in other ways, I know at least one person will find great value in the insights I have shared in this book. These stepping stones in life are part of a natural growth and progression; they exude the mindset of being a student of life, for life.

**It is not what you get from the learning, it is what you become that matters!**

With each new thing I learn, I become better in some manner. Sometimes this "better" is personal in the way of knowledge, compassion, and understanding. At other times, the "better" is for others by understanding their needs better and helping them navigate what they must to grow their business, grow as a person, or find a great merger between their authentic selves and their business sense. Whatever it is, contributing to others helps me continue growing right along with them. I love this type of energy and engagement with others.

Learning for the sake of learning is powerful; however, learning about something because it will help you contribute even more to the world will give your learning meaning. It's the spice of life! The opposite of learning and growth is stagnation, entropy, and death. Personally, I have enjoyed learning about world history, including Greek mythology and its famous philosophers, such as Socrates and Aristotle. There are great personal lessons to be learned in the wisdom of the Bible. A hobby, as well as a necessity for me has been learning to cook, so I enjoy reading cookbooks too. Nothing is off-limits because the more I know, the more empowered I become to find and experience joy. Sometimes that joy comes from learning in areas I never would have suspected to be interesting (philosophy, for example). Some of my most exciting moments have come from learning during my travels!

You may be asking, how do these topics help me contribute to the world? Independently, not much, but in concert all these subjects have opened my mind to new ways of approaching challenges and have without doubt helped me connect better with people from all walks of life. I am now more capable of connection with people from many different backgrounds with a variety of interests. Finding common interests with interesting people has enriched my life and theirs equally.

**You never know where a conversation is going to take you, but if your knowledge is limited, you know where it will end.**

In the end, this all comes down to honoring a sense of personal joy and fulfillment within you. When you feel rooted in knowledge, you can be open and accessible to others, as well as a source of wisdom that others can turn to when they desire to do so.

It excites me to know that by being a student of life, I cannot grow stagnant. Being a student of life is not about being a doctor or having a high pedigree; it is about looking at the world with eyes of wonderment. What is that? How does it work? What can I learn from this? The wisest people I've ever met contemplate these questions about everything they encounter. With or without a formal education, wisdom seems to attract success in any profession.

**Every aspect of my life has become better since I have learned that communication helps bridge the gaps and differences that people have. Without learning that, I would have been doing a great disservice to my life and to those I meet as well.**

It's exciting to see how I can take a weakness, even on a topic I don't particularly enjoy, and tackle it. Those challenges are exciting. One challenge for me has been with communication. Everyone agrees that good communication is important in any type of relationship. I have always taken pride in my ability to express my thoughts and feelings well, but then why was I not communicating well with some of the people closest to me? I am now the father of one teenager and another soon to be. I know it has been 28 years since I was a teenager, but I wouldn't have imagined I would struggle to communicate effectively with one. Especially one that is my son. Turns out I needed to become a better listener, particularly for those topics where I perhaps disagree. Although I was able to express myself well, I found out it is just as important to do so succinctly and specifically. Since practice makes improvement, I have committed to the practice of listening and continue to work on the skills that will make me a more effective communicator, especially with teenagers!

## REFLECTIVE EXERCISE

The key to gaining knowledge is to understand those areas in which you struggle. That is why this reflective exercise will take you into that with which you are most uncomfortable—those moments where you interact with people you disagree with or don't understand. This is definitely a hot topic in today's heated political climate, which is why it is necessary.

Take some time to think about those conversations that have really made you feel uncomfortable, whether years ago or yesterday. You know that you remember them. Think about your responses…

1. Were you really listening? When did you stop listening?
2. If you found yourself bored or uncomfortable, you likely were not equipped with the knowledge to contribute. Start by listing these deficiencies so you can start your education.
   - Create a fascination with that topic and learning in general.
   - Be excited to learn every day.
3. Were you already thinking of your rebuttal while the other person was still speaking?
4. How much were your emotions involved in your perspective?
5. Did you walk away with a better understanding, or did you double down on your current stance?

Remember, you don't have to agree with someone to understand them better. That is not a requirement. When awkward or disagreeable situations arise, it can feel difficult, and let's face it, it is much easier for us to feel someone else is wrong than to admit we may be wrong or lack the knowledge. That takes work, and it emphasizes a natural desire to grow wiser and more discerning.

*   *   *

When we care about others and the human condition, we are required to become good listeners. That is the foundation of all growth. By listening objectively and not casting judgment, we can become the person that others open up to and respect. When you truly listen to others you will be amazed at the things you learn.

# ONLY COWARDS DO WHAT THEY CAN

"With courage you will dare to take risks, have the strength to be compassionate, and the wisdom to be humble. Courage is the foundation of integrity."

– MARK TWAIN

749,000 was the price tag on a house one block away from the home I lived in with my kids. At this point, their mother still lived with us, but our relationship was obviously over. I insisted with a lot of passion she buy the home and offered to give her the down payment so that she could live near me as we would surely split custody of the boys when she moved out. She of course refused to consider the purchase, so I looked into buying it myself. At this point, I owed $560,000 on the mortgage of my home and owed $330,000 from my school loans yet the banks seemed willing to let me borrow more money. When reviewing the numbers and my monthly payments I was a little intimidated and since we are being honest, I was afraid. Afraid to take on more debt and not be able to pay. After some difficult deliberation, I decided NOT to move forward with the purchase. Only 2 years later that same home was for sale again for $1.5 million! Fear got the best of me. I lost out on three quarters of a million dollars and worst of all my sons were not near me when they were with their mother!

### Becoming mature enough to be self-aware and understand your shortcomings is important work to undertake.

I am still ashamed to admit this is how I dealt with my situation! Not long after the birth of my second son, it was obvious to me that my relationship with their mother was not going to last. Truthfully, she and I had very different ideas of how we wanted our lives to progress, and I was not mature or self-aware enough to understand my shortcomings as a partner to accept what seemed like ridiculous demands from her. That is not what I am ashamed of because I eventually put in the work to overcome my most detrimental faults as a partner. What I am ashamed of was the way I dragged out the termination of that relationship, hurting a lot of people in the process. Instead of facing our inevitable split head-on, in complete cowardice I simply stopped communicating with her and continued to coexist in the same house. Looking back, I was more afraid of not being under the same roof with my sons every day than I was about asking her to move out of my home. In an attempt to move on with my life, I started dating other women while the mother of my kids continued to live under the same roof with me. Sure, she was dating as well, and as long as we stayed out of one another's way everything seemed calm on the surface. As you can imagine, those circumstances simply drove us further and further away which is a horrible thing when we were raising two young boys (4 and 1.5 years old at that time).

It all came to a head when one day the mother of my kids saw text messages from another woman meant for me on my son's iPad. I had forgotten we shared the same iCloud account! I am sure she already knew this was happening but seeing it must have been very traumatic and upsetting because that led to a series of very dramatic events that I will spare you the painful details of. Suffice to say that at my lowest point I was escorted by police out of my own home when her anger caused her to lie to the police and tell them I had "pushed her to the ground." All charges were dropped after an investigation, but that shameful event led me to look at myself as the cause of all this drama and anguish.

Only in retrospect can I see that it was fear of the unknown that led to inaction. It was fear of losing my home, my seemingly perfect image of what someone successful should have, fear that no one else would want me, fear that I was not loveable, fear that I would not have a reason to be frustrated and disappointed by my relationship because it was exactly those emotions that drove me to dedicate my efforts toward my kids and my career.

**By admitting that I'd let fear paralyze my decision-making process and results, I was able to begin learning how to harness my fear and experience the liberation of replacing cowardice with better choices.**

Fear can be all-consuming and at times it can be paralyzing. It does seem easier not to act, not decide, not confront the uncomfortable truths so that everything we know remains the same. This fear is about not knowing if we can handle the challenges an unknown tomorrow will bring. And the root cause of that fear is not knowing that we already have the tools to face and grow through any challenge. The truth is most of us do already have a robust tool belt in the arsenal our life experiences have given us, but we just haven't yet learned how to access it at will.

**"The only things you learn are the things you tame."**

– ANTOINE DE SAINT-EXUPERY, THE LITTLE PRINCE

Have you ever watched as a truly skilled craftsman creates? I recently watched a sculptor work on a project with a very fragile material. Nearly 60 hours of work into this project the material he is working with fails and fractures at a critical point in the piece. Without hesitation, the craftsman throws out the fractured portion and immediately starts reshaping the remaining material to create something completely different yet outstanding in its own right. When the project was done, he was asked, "Are you happy with the outcome? How much did that material failure when you were nearly done impact your workflow, idea, and outcome?" The craftsman said calmly and with complete confidence, "In art just like life, things don't always turn out as we plan them. The key to success is not being fixed on a specific outcome, but instead creating the best possible product with whatever you must work with."

## REFLECTIVE EXERCISE

The key to not acting cowardly and moving forward with courage is being able to identify when fear is driving your actions. As soon as you do, pause and evaluate your decision-making.

1. Is what you fear real?
2. Does the fear serve you in some way?
3. What is the fear keeping you from?
4. What will happen if you act against that fear?

> When I start feeling challenged by fear or when I stop moving forward, I pause and run through these questions. This is what I want you to do next time you are being stopped or slowed down by fear.
> - What is holding you back?
> - Why are you inactive?
> - What is the worst that could happen if I do act?
> - Really, what are you afraid of? Because most of the time, it is a fear of something intangible or imagined. Once you understand your fears you are free to harness them and, most importantly, move past them.

Our tendency as humans is to protect ourselves from failure and pain. That is the ego's goal anyhow. The ego is playing a wicked game on you and this reaction prevents progress. Overcoming the fears that hinder the pursuit of your best life or outcome is one of the greatest rewards you can give yourself.

# BE THE MASTER OF YOUR TIME

"It's not enough to be busy, so
are the ants. The question is,
what are we busy about?"

– HENRY DAVID THOREAU

Have you ever said, "Where does the time go?" I have heard people say this quite often. I may have even asked that question myself. For many years I had no control over my time. My mindset was one of insufficiency and like in Principle #14, I reacted and made decisions based on the fear that I never had enough time. This mentality pushed me into being one of those people who were always running around looking busy but without clear direction. I came from a background of poverty and constant economic struggle so turning down work was a sin to me. I was also afraid that if I declined work or invitations to just about anything then those people would forget me the next time there was an opportunity. I became the ultimate "yes" man and found myself working 24/7, sleep-deprived, and with little enjoyment in my work or quality of life.

Can you take this on? Yes!

Will you finish this for me? Yes!

Hey, let's do a triathlon! Sure! It didn't matter that I didn't really know how to swim; I was too afraid to say no and thought I would figure it out. So what if had no idea what I was committing to in the moment!

With all these yeses, the time commitments were making it impossible for me to see that an occasional "no" would be beneficial. I was overburdened and time deficient, and as a result, I stopped being deliberate about my actions. I became so consumed with making good on my commitments that I could not enjoy the beautiful moments these endeavors offered. The absolute worst part of it is that I couldn't prioritize those things which were most important to me. I was also consumed with making it to the next commitment, so I was never fully present in the present moment.

I remember the day that I first noticed my way of approaching life just wasn't working out for me. As usual, I was at a meeting with someone who had another amazing opportunity for me. Sadly, I had postponed this meeting a couple of times because I was "so busy," but at last I was sitting with this old acquaintance. She went on to say that she believed

I was perfect for this venture as a partner, but she had by now decided to go in a different direction. Naturally, I asked why that was. She told me it wasn't personal, but I obviously had too much going on and she needed a partner who could commit and be mentally present to help launch this business. Perhaps it wasn't personal to her, but it felt like I'd been kicked below the belt. Those words, for some reason, struck a chord and hurt more deeply than they should have.

Hearing this was so painful for two reasons. Number one, what she said was true, and number two, I realized that I had to find a way to be more deliberate about my time and commitments so that I could dedicate my time to major things, and, most importantly, be completely present in every moment. Another day was too long to wait for change. The awareness of this flaw made me angry with myself and that fueled the courage to change immediately.

Realizing this, the question became: where should I dedicate my time? How do I prioritize my commitments? Business had been the excuse for so long that it was a challenge to escape its grasp. I had to gain clarity about my priorities and find ways to dedicate my time to what mattered most. NO, had to become my new sense of security. I changed my mindset completely and started rejecting all offers and would only change my mind once a thorough evaluation process had been completed making sure it met every requirement to make my priority list.

**I needed a plan that would help me assess what I should do to master my time and results on a daily, weekly, or even monthly basis.**

Focusing on things that "move the needle" is a good way to start. This means I have to know what my primary objective is so that I can consider which activities are the most beneficial in helping me achieve such a goal. Once I have my priorities aligned, living in the moment and giving my best effort becomes second nature.

Learning how to say NO is a big step in time management, but there are simpler ways to make strides immediately resulting in more fulfilling daily outcomes. Limiting my time on social media is one of the biggest factors that freed up a lot of time. It is so easy to lose track of time and get distracted on social media. Watching television is another thing that can get out of control. Getting emotionally caught up in a Netflix series could monopolize days of my life! Personally, I don't watch TV, but if you do, make sure it is the last thing you do after your tasks are done. Additionally, quality time with kids and family is better than staring at a TV screen, and I have never felt regret about spending any amount of time with my family.

**When you're a busy individual, it is impossible to be 100 percent at all things, which means that you must shift your priorities to keep making consistent progress toward your goals.**

Don't beat yourself up when you realize that what you are dedicating your time to isn't helping your cause as you thought it would. Shifting your priorities and setting that aside to change direction is ok. This doesn't mean you wasted your time, but instead you eliminated one more possibility. You learned what doesn't work and quickly moved on to something else. Sounds easy, doesn't it? Once again, I must be the bearer of bad news. It is NOT easy at all. The biggest challenge I encountered in this process was accepting the changes to all my relationships as my priorities shifted. Learning to let go of the relationships that no longer served me allowed me the flexibility to grow into my new mindset. This system is not rigid, and can therefore work for you just as it has worked for me. This adaptability fused with your mentality leads to a sense of freedom. Freedom to move in any direction at any time, or simply stand back and take a break, allows you to breathe deeply, appreciate the process, and, most of all, trust the process.

Don't forget, when you fail to protect your time, others will always step in and decide how you spend it for you.

## REFLECTIVE EXERCISE

Every person on this planet gets the same amount of time every day! That is a very important fact to remember. So how can you become more effective with your time? The only way is to manage those 24 hours more wisely. Does not matter if you are a stay-at-home parent or a busy professional. It's all about balance, and time management is synonymous with life management.

To start the process of gaining control over my output of time, I began a routine that has never failed, and I believe it will work for you.

1.  On Sunday nights, I look ahead to my upcoming week (both with personal and professional commitments) and list what I need to accomplish for the week.

2.  Next, I prioritize that list into what must get done, what I would like to get done, and those things that would be helpful in some way to get done. This is where it gets tricky because only you can decide what is valuable for you and is aligned with your goals and what is more busy work that can be delegated, automated, or eliminated.

3.  The last step I take is to decide how much time you will dedicate daily to each task. That means that when your time is up you must stop and move on to the next task. If along the way you see that one task needs more time than anticipated, you must decide which other task to deprioritize and take time from. This is the reason that time is the most valuable resource because you will never get more than twenty-four hours a day.

Then, as you do your tasks, you can start crossing them off when they are complete and evaluating if:

- You were accurate with the estimated time
- Is your priority list accurate? (Is it helping you move towards your goal)
- Are any of these task's reoccurring? If so, can it be automated or delegated?

Reassess if you're making progress or if you need to shift your priorities.

You can further break down these tasks into those that are professional in nature and those that are personal, such as family. I like to break down my schedule into work, family, and leisure (family and leisure often flow over into each other). This way, I know what I am doing and the value I am getting in actions has a net positive return in my life. Doing this has made me less stressed, more productive, happier, and more positively engaged with my family. Those are big wins!

\* \* \*

We make some of the biggest mistakes when we dedicate a lot of time to a task but don't act with focus and purpose. Even smart, successful people are susceptible to this. It's finding the way to merge personal lives with professional success that becomes problematic. By paying attention to how we use our time, we will always have the right amount of time to devote to those things we care about most.

# THERE IS NO SUCH THING AS UNCONDITIONAL LOVE

"Giving and receiving love is vital to human existence. It is the glue that binds couples, families, communities, cultures, and nations."

– G. FRANK LAWLIS

How many times have you heard someone romanticize "true love?" If I had a dime for every time I heard someone say, "I want that unconditional love only a baby of my own or a dog can offer!" This is a big point of contention for me because I strongly disagree that unconditional love exists. I am a believer that many people have misunderstood love and what it really means. It is easy to confuse the ideal love with unconditional love. Our ideal love varies from one person to another just like our favorite ice cream flavor, but one thing holds true: we all have a unique image of what our ideal love looks and feels like.

Being a human means having certain conditions, especially in love. Let's take what I consider the purest type of love, love for your children. Most people would say that there was nothing their children could do or say that would diminish their love for them. As a parent myself I can attest there are many times when my patience is challenged by my teenage son, and many times we don't like one another much. There are times when I as a parent feel unappreciated and ignored by my children. There have been instances when I am frustrated beyond belief with my children, but never has my love diminished. On the contrary, I feel more love for them with every passing moment. However, that love comes with conditions.

As you know I have two sons, who are now 14 and 11 years old, whom I have raised to be strong independent free thinkers. This was on purpose, but at times that spirit frustrates me to my breaking point. I have found myself sounding just like my parents when I was kid. "Don't question me! Do as I say simply because I say so!" Those are phrases I used to despise as a child and vowed to never repeat with my children, yet I have on more than one occasion. After a few deep breaths and resetting my patience gauge, it is easy to recognize they are being kids and challenging me is normal.

These encounters do not change how much I love them, but they do highlight that I have certain expectations. Reciprocation of respect love and effort is the minimum of what I expect from my kids. As much as I love them, there is a breaking point when that patience my love allows is challenged. Love always comes with conditions but accepting that helps define conditions that are reasonable. Once I understood that, I was finally able to appreciate giving and receiving love freely, even if it was with reciprocal conditions.

**Abundant love does not come at the cost of conceding your value and dignity.**

All of life's relationships should be viewed this way. It is within the beauty of those conditions and understanding that you show love to yourself while laying out the foundation of your life to those who are going to be a part of it—the givers and recipients of love in your life.

It's not my place to judge, but we all realize that there are certain conditions under which others love us more. This is likely why I spend so much time and energy learning how to be a better listener, more thoughtful, more empathetic, and better in tune with the love languages of those closest to me. It may be completely selfish, but YES, I want them to love me more! It is just as important to understand the conditions under which we also love ourselves more. It is ridiculous when you say it out loud, but that is just the way it is. When you understand this, you experience a whole lot of freedom to be yourself and treat yourself as well as you do your loved ones.

"When a poet digs himself a hole, he doesn't
climb out. He digs deeper, enjoys the scenery, and
comes out of the other side enlightened."

— CRISS JAMI, VENUS IN ARMS

When it comes to romantic love, I am not the best model of
success. What I have to offer comes from the lessons I have learned
from my failures. The first time I fell in love I was 5 years old, and
it was on my first bus ride to my first day of kindergarten. This
beautiful girl asked me to share a seat with her and by the time we
arrived at school we were holding hands. When I was 8, I fell in love
with my third-grade teacher. She was 24 years old, smart, tall, and
gorgeous. That fascination ended when I met her fiancé. After that
huge disappointment, I did not feel love again until college. I fell
for my next-door neighbor because she smelled so good and was
so different from me. Our relationship evolved and despite its ups
and downs, we were married to meet our goals of starting a family
by our 30th birthday. For painful reasons that I will spare you from,
we were divorced three and a half years later. Not long after my
divorce, I met the mother of my kids and in the aftermath of such
a failure she was quickly pregnant. I never married her but as you
have already heard earlier in this book, that relationship soon failed
as well. The romantic love I have found since has also come with its
challenges and stumbles. Ultimately, the common denominator in
these failed relationships has been me. After much reflection and
introspection, my conclusion was that my failures all came down to
the same reason. My lack of maturity and understanding of my own
limitations made me a bad romantic partner. I was looking to others
to fill a void in my life. I didn't feel I was enough and demanded my
partners to fill that need. Even if they were able to love me at their
capacity, I wasn't ready to accept that love. Because I felt insufficient,
I gave so much of myself to my partners and didn't spend the time

to learn to love myself in the same manner. That led me to feel that my partners didn't love me and would never give me the same efforts I was extending them. It is not until now that I understand it was my inability to love myself that prevented me from accepting the love I was offered.

**In love, just like most things in life, you will rarely be met halfway.**

My father has always been an amazing dad. He gave me his all and continues to do so until this very day. I can't say I will ever be able to give him as much love as he has given me. Maybe that is how he feels about his father, but from what I knew of my granddad's relationship with my dad I didn't feel that was the case. Only a few years ago my grandfather passed away, and since we were not close, I didn't feel compelled to attend the funeral. I also resented my grandfather for not appreciating the great man that was his son and my father. Still, this funeral mattered to my dad, and he was devastated by the loss. Despite my feelings about my grandfather, I knew I needed to be there for my dad. I took a week off work and spent it supporting my dad through his grief. I'll never regret that because it brought us closer than ever. I have no doubt that my dad felt the love I was extending him. I was also able to appreciate how much my dad loved his father despite his flaws. Even in his grief, he taught me that love isn't exchanged like money in fair trade. Love should be given and accepted like charitable donations: in any form it is offered.

**Stop and evaluate how you feel about your actions. If your driving force is primarily love, the outcome will always be favorable.**

Contemplating your intentions is an important part of love. If you start these internal dialogues with statements such as "If I do this, maybe they will do that," you are likely not allowing love to steer you. I am not saying that the barter system won't produce results, it is simply that results tend to be short-lived and dissatisfying in the long run. It becomes much more rewarding and satisfying when we change our philosophy to something like this, "I will give and do because I love to help and serve everyone I encounter. Having a positive impact on others is all the reward I need."

If the common adage about true love being selfless is accurate, we need to start being more aware of how we love others and, even more importantly, how we love ourselves.

## REFLECTIVE EXERCISE

Although difficult, I find this reflective exercise to be enlightening and stimulating. It is because most of our failed relationships tend to come down to unfulfilled expectations, and, as we learned in this chapter, those feelings are usually misplaced. Lets evaluate how fair those expectations are:

Take some time to dive into situations you have been involved in that left you feeling disappointed and dig into these thoughts:

- What were my expectations in this relationship or situation?
- What was my contribution to that situation or relationship?
- Were my actions based in love or was it transactional?
- If this relationship/situation had worked out to perfection, what would that have looked like?
- What could I have done personally to ensure that perfect outcome?
- Is it possible that an amazing love was offered, but you were unable to accept it?
- Do you love yourself as much or more than you love those closest to you?

I find ideal love to be elusive because in our culture we are taught to love others beyond how we love ourselves. This is obvious by the things we will do for others and not ourselves. For that same reason we tend to depend on others to fill that void the lack of self-love leaves. That in turn leads to big disappointments and failed relationships. In my case, it was never that I believed I wasn't deserving my own love, but that I believed the measure of my love was directly correlated with my sacrifices for others. It took me more than forty years of living through failures to learn that I could not accept the love I expected until I learned to love myself just as much as I do others.

# LEARN TO PIVOT

"Before a dream can mature
and manifest itself as real, a
lot of loaded efforts come into
play! You are the pivot on which
those loads must be turned!"

– ISRAELMORE AYIVOR

When I was a child, I wanted more than anything to become an astronaut! Math and science were intuitive to me, which gave me hope of achieving that huge aspiration. I used to think, play, and even dream about piloting a shuttle into space! I will never forget that moment in 1986 when my entire school gathered in the gym to watch the launch of The Challenger into space! I am sure everyone in the world was impacted by its tragic outcome, but for me the traumatic impact of that tragedy filled my dream with fear and challenged my resolve. I was able to overcome that fear in time and continued to dream about a future in which the universe was my playground. Sadly, by the time I was in high school my eyesight had failed me and I required corrective lenses, so I was disqualified from ever being a pilot. As my eyesight continued to get worse my dreams of piloting a space shuttle dwindled, but deep inside I still believe I will make it to space one day.

**The decisions a person makes when they must pivot are massive because they require you to release the old dream and embrace the new opportunity.**

So being an astronaut was out of the realm of possibilities, but I was not about to just lay down in self-pity! I had other passions. As you read in earlier chapters, I grew up a chubby kid. I didn't particularly enjoy being that way, so I was driven to do something about it. This drive forced me to learn about exercise and, more importantly, the value of nutrition. Nutrition and the science behind it quickly became a passion for me. I devoured as much information as I could find and began to experiment with dietary changes and supplements on myself. I tried all sorts of nutrition schemes, some of which were extreme and questioned as crazy by my family, but I learned a lot. This fascination led me to becoming a personal trainer and helping others improve their lifestyle to be healthier.

The ability to help people live healthier lives and seeing my clients succeed under my guidance generated an excitement I hadn't felt before. After a little research and some guidance, I had found the pivot that would define the rest of my life. The University of California at Davis had the number one Nutrition Science program in the country at the time, so I would now shift my sights there to become a nutrition scientist. What do those professionals do?" asked my parents. I would use that degree to catapult me to a PhD in Nutrition Science with the ultimate goal being the NIH. The National Institute of Health, where I would help the charge against childhood obesity (which was starting to become a pandemic in our country).

You must be thinking, "wait, isn't he a medical doctor?" Yes, I am. Along my path at UC Davis, my then mentor pulled me aside and wanted to speak as friends. He went on to tell me he had honestly appreciated getting to know me over my time at UC Davis, and although I would be great as a PhD my gift would be grossly underutilized in a lab. He said I was "a people person," and I should consider medicine as a career choice. His argument was that as a doctor I could still make an impact on childhood obesity but have direct patient contact which he believed was my gift: connecting with people. I took his advice and after an amazing experience as a volunteer in the hospital at UC Davis medical center, I applied to medical schools. Fortunately, a few schools saw my potential and accepted me.

I went into medicine with an open mind and a heart full of love for helping as many people as I could. My first real clinical experience as a third-year medical student was with a cardiothoracic surgeon, Dr. Nuno, who was one of the very few Mexican physicians in that field. He was strong, smart, direct, and bold. Watching him open a chest, stop the heart, repair it, and restart it was amazing! He was a man anyone could respect. After only a week of working with him, he asked me to rethink if cardiothoracic surgery was the path I wished to take. Of course, I asked why? He shared that he had to work a lot harder than everyone else to achieve the goal. The path required all of his time and effort. He had sacrificed so much, including his family and friends, and now the world didn't even appreciate his skills. He was resentful that every year he was paid less for his services and, in his opinion, it was NOT worth the sacrifice.

I am not afraid of hard work or putting in the time it takes to succeed; however, I am very aware of the value I place on my time and family. I eliminated cardiothoracic surgery immediately. As I experienced different specialties in medicine, I changed my career path several times. I ended up in the family medicine program at UC San Diego Medical Center, which seemed to offer the best balance of career and quality of life.

The excitement and enthusiasm with which I started my residency program at UCSD medical center could not have been greater. I wish I could tell you the experience was amazing and had a fairy tale ending, but of course that is the opposite of the truth. Soon after the start of the program, it was obvious that hard work and enthusiasm for patient care was not the formula for acceptance in the academic setting of the residency program. Once again, I just didn't fit the mold. I just couldn't fall in line and meet the sociopolitical expectations of the program.

I survived the program only by the merits of my work ethic. It seemed obvious I had to be my own boss, or I would always find difficulties. Unlike most of my classmates, I started my own business right out of training and started doing whatever I could to pay the bills. This included seeing patients in their homes, nursing homes, and even filling in at clinics for doctors that needed a break on occasion. This strategy worked for several years. I was making a lot of money, but it came at a cost. When I found myself part of a system that was not aligned with my ethics or goals, I was once again forced to pivot. Those details you have already read in previous chapters, but to remind you this last pivot brought me to the incredible satisfaction and freedom I now thrive in!

# "IN THE MIDDLE OF DIFFICULTY LIES OPPORTUNITY."

## – ALBERT EINSTEIN

If I am truly living, there will never come a time when I don't have to pivot anymore. I view the pivot as proof of progress. Because I am a student of life for life, I will continue to outgrow my current dreams and goals. I will continue to challenge my beliefs and having the flexibility to pivot is necessary for growth. I don't want to miss opportunities to grow, experience, laugh, and love. I enjoy being on a better path every day and aligning myself with good things that are yet to come - situations I may not even know about yet. Being less rigid resonates well with me and allows me to look forward to the future with excitement. Without curiosity, progress, and a good portion of uncertainty there is little to look forward to.

## REFLECTIVE EXERCISE

As you have seen in this chapter, the ability to pivot is essential in your path to freedom. If you are already 100 percent satisfied with your perfect life then no need to go any further, but because most of us are not I urge you to try the exercise below:

- Am I on a path of my free choice, or am I trying to please somebody else?
- Am I satisfied with my journey? And is my direction clear?
- Am I feeling a little lost in my path? And if so, how have I ended up at this point?
- Have I missed potentially desirable opportunities because I was rigid in my beliefs and was afraid to change my mind?
- If I am not 100 percent sure about my path or even my ideal goal, why? What would my journey feel like if I was 100 percent sure of my goal or destination?
- Are you waiting for THE ONE clear path? It is better to choose a destination and set sail than to wait in uncertainty for the right path. PIVOT as much as needed but keep making progress.

\* \* \*

Knowing you can pivot anywhere along your path is liberating. Do not fear growth. Develop the skills you may need, commit the time it takes, and make your actions matter. This is how you prevent unnecessary suffering and find joy in everything you do.

# BE PREPARED FOR TRANSCENDENCE

"To recognize one's own insanity is, of course, the arising of sanity, the beginning of healing and transcendence."

– ECKHART TOLLE

Leaving behind the safety of familiarity is NOT easy. To transcend one's socioeconomic limits can be emotionally difficult. This step means we are outgrowing the people and environment we were born into and that have shaped our lives until this point. There is an inherent risk that some of the people closest to you will see you in a different light and likely demonstrate hurt feelings and resentment. The same people whom you love and trust may start projecting their own insecurities upon you and say things like, "now you think you are better than me?" There is also a very real risk that you may sabotage your own progress when you realize that you are no longer connecting to your people as your goals change and your mind opens to the universe's potential.

Look at me. I started out in a tiny cabin rented from the owner of the farm my parents worked on. This small community still exists today in almost the exact same conditions as it did 40 years ago when I lived there. A lot of the same families remain there still and have no aspirations to grow past their circumstances. This reality was never as evident until I brought my sons to see where I spent the first 9 years of my life. The loving memories were all still there, but the gratitude for my parents' strength to move on and allow my growth filled my heart.

**It did not take long for me to realize that once I left that environment, I wasn't going back. My thoughts didn't stem from thinking I was better than those people who stayed behind. They were a product of seeing more closely all the amazing things that existed in the world beyond the boundaries of that farm.**

I was so scared when we first moved to our new home that was in town and thirty miles away from the farm that I so dearly loved. Thirty miles felt like a universe away! The fear of our new surroundings was so real and intense. I no longer trusted my neighbors. Everyone seemed to always be in a hurry and living such independent lives.

This was everything that my first 9 years of life were not. It wasn't until one weekend only about a month into our new home when my mom, my dad, my brother, and I were all home together and had a chance to share our fears. My mother cried and confessed that every single day she wished we could go back to our little cabin on the farm. My brother and I cried with her and quickly agreed we should return. It was my father, with his calm and common sense, that spoke with confidence and reminded us that this was our home, that we were fortunate to be able to own our home, and that in time we would grow accustomed to our new surroundings. In his usual brief but strong fashion, he reminded us that as long as we were together as a family, we had nothing to fear and that he had no doubt this home was the best decision for our family.

My parents realized that we were taking a necessary step to help me, and my siblings grow. We knew there wasn't any real physical danger to fear; we were experiencing grief for leaving a life we had enjoyed so much.

### "Transcendence constitutes selfhood."

– MARTIN HEIDEGGER

When I reflect on how many different communities I have established residence in, thrived in, contributed to, and then transcended I feel grateful for their contribution to the person I am today. My thirty-year class reunion has recently taken place. My high school class had nine hundred kids in it when I was a freshman. Of that number, only 189 graduated. And out of that 189, I was the only Latino in the top 5 percent of the graduating class. I went on to fulfill my dream of lifelong progress, but most everyone I grew up with did not have that same fortune.

I left home the summer after high school graduation, and I was once again so afraid. Afraid to leave my family, friends, and the community which loved and accepted me exactly as I was. Luckily that fear was not greater than my reasons for leaving. I knew I had outgrown that environment. Most of the kids I saw grow up there ended up as teenage parents and were forced to enter the workforce to support their families. Those were the fortunate ones. Others got involved in gangs, which were very prominent in that community, and ended up in prison or dead. There was no doubt I had to leave this community and expand my mind if I was to exceed the expectations for young men where I grew up. Although I have more education and world experience than most of my family and people I grew up with, I have never forgotten my roots and their role in my success.

**No matter how wealthy you become or how much you transcend your origins, the genuine essence of your being will always be evident.**

Recently, I attended a family reunion for the holidays. I was so excited to see some of my family members that had been lost to me for years. When I arrived, I learned from my mother what everyone did to prepare for my arrival. Since I was a doctor, they assumed I was a completely changed person and they would be held to different standards by me. They were frantic with cleaning and making sure everything was done to a high level to impress me. In reality, we hugged, shared and laughed at old stories, enjoyed our favorite traditional foods together, and ultimately found the bond that we created when I was a child had not changed at all. They later shared, with some shame, that it was a shock to them that my personality and energy towards them had not changed a bit. They had been afraid that my "success" would have changed my ability to connect with them- that is their own words. They complimented kindly about how I was still the same humble and nice person they remembered growing up with. In my heart, I wouldn't be me without their contribution to my upbringing, and I will forever love them and be grateful.

**Everyone can outgrow their limiting beliefs without outgrowing the people who are a part of their lives.**

In my life, I have been dissatisfied with the lack of progress over the previous two generations before me. Growing up, I couldn't believe that even with ten siblings no one in my dad's family had taken the initiative to set greater standards in education and business within our family. It seemed everyone was ok with just following the same path as their predecessors. I cannot recall when that complacency began to bother me, but I can remember clearly that by the time I was 10 years old I decided that it was up to me to change my family's tranjectory.

I soon became the first in our family to graduate high school on the traditional path. I say this because there may be one or two older cousins who have gone back to school later to complete a GED (general education degree-High School Equivalent) before I finished high school. I was definitely the first in our family to successfully finish a four-year college degree and go on to get a Doctor of Medicine. Since my accomplishments, many of my cousins have gone to college and some have successfully completed master's degrees. I am sharing this not to brag, but on the contrary to show that one's personal growth can be a positive catalyst for the whole. Also, to show that it is a personal choice to transcend and forget or to transcend and include your loved ones in that growth.

## REFLECTIVE EXERCISE

It is very helpful to identify your reasons for wanting to grow and transcend your current situation.

The scary part of transcendence is you may feel that you are required to leave the things or people that define you behind. Be assured that this is not a requirement for transcendence. Sometimes those closest to you can unintentionally hinder your transcendence. They may just be trying to protect you from failure or pain, but that is them projecting their own fears onto you. They could just be protecting themselves from the fear of losing you.

This fear stems from a dialogue embedded in your roots and possibly an unhealthy attachment to all aspects of them. For me, I am still attached to the people I care about from my youth, but I am not to the limits that my roots may indicate I should have.

To master transcendence, you need to master your fears. Ponder the following and answer truthfully:

- What are the things in life that are difficult to accept personally? Shyness, failure, and passiveness are three examples (of many). Anything that holds you back can be difficult to accept.
- Are limiting beliefs impacting the joy and flow of your life? Limiting beliefs are tied to your sense of self-worth and self-confidence; both qualities benefit your best life.
- What about your current situation frustrates or angers you?
- Is there a person or community which anchors you, but you suspect you are outgrowing?
- Do you fear moving forward past your current state even if your current situation is not your ideal? This often happens when people contemplate the unknown, even when those thoughts are positive. There is a fear of success…that is a real thing.

- Do you want to forget the past? Or can you honor the people and situations of your past as you transcend into your best future?

Once you acknowledge that you have the right to grow past any situation or circumstance, and you can do so while bringing those you love most with you, it becomes much easier to move past anything that you have outgrown.

*   *   *

Remember that life is not just about achieving for yourself. Transcending for the greater good allows you the opportunity to do something inspirational.

# EVOLVE INTO THE TRUE YOU

"If you can't fly, then run; If you can't run, then walk: If you can't walk, then crawl: but whatever you do, you have to keep moving forward."

– MARIN LUTHER KING JR.

Let's start with this simple fact: evolution is a process. It does not happen in a day; it takes time, really an entire lifetime. As we have discussed throughout this book, if we are really living evolution should be lifelong.

As we learned in Chapter 17: Learn to Pivot, changing directions at any time is essential for success. Pivoting can be fast, and agility is essential, but evolution is slow and deliberate. It took me a solid two years to make the biggest shift of my adult life.

It was February 1, 2018. I woke up feeling fed up with my own dissatisfaction. I decided to quit everything, including my job. Now I am not saying that was smart or the only way to pivot, but that is the catalyst I chose to encourage the evolutionary process. I had six months of money reserves to live on, and no real plan on how I would generate money anytime soon. All the work that had consumed me 24/7/365 ended. No more calls, text messages, or emergency messages at all hours of the night. My phone went dead, and since that was the source of my livelihood for so long, it was extremely disconcerting when it all stopped.

Then my "What did I do?" moment set in. Nobody was looking for me anymore and it was by my own decision. So now I had no more excuses. It was time to work toward becoming the best person I could be. It was time to make progress toward the dream I started as a child.

I began to educate myself with books and seminars and I devoured as much information as I could to help me improve my knowledge base and refine my skills. Most days I was cool, calm, and collected knowing I was on the right path. Some days my calm demeanor dissipated, and I began to panic as I thought about the near future and the lack of resources, I would soon find myself with. There were thoughts about my sons and providing for them and a tremendous amount of uncertainty as to what my future may look like. I had no idea where I was ultimately headed, but I knew it had to be the opposite of where I was on February 1, 2018.

Every morning began with meditation and self-talk reassuring myself I was on the right path. It was vital that I started each day believing that I was 100 percent in on my goals. All I had to do the rest of the day was trust the process. Sounds easy! After meditation, I would read for 20 minutes. Any book on self-help I had at the moment because I had a lot of learning and growing to do if I was to make any progress. I followed that with an intense workout that was sure to clear my mind of any doubts and leave me feeling accomplished, at least physically. I spent the middle of my days learning from mentors, people who seemed to be where I wanted to go, about business and mindset. I ended every day writing down my daily highlights, what I learned, and my own reflective exercises. Some days, it was about shortcomings, and other days, it was about strategy and action. Still, time was at a premium, and I couldn't afford to waste a second.

> **"Wisdom is knowing what to do next, skill is knowing how to do it, and virtue is doing it."**
>
> – DAVID STAR JORDAN

Slowly, priorities started to emerge from what I discovered about myself, and they became my plan of action. I squeezed as much time into a day as I possibly could and still made time for my sons. Over the first 6 months, I clarified my purpose and found meaning in my actions. This forward progression felt good, although it didn't always keep me safe from doubts about my success or the fear of a complete meltdown. I also had frustrating moments where I couldn't see my progress and I had to find ways to refocus my attention during those critical sink-or-swim times.

Having confidence in my beliefs made a big difference. Even though I was more broke than anything else, I experienced a sign that I was on the right track that year. At Christmas, my sons and I were opening presents. There were not a lot of gifts because, for the first time since finishing my medical education, I couldn't afford them. Yet, there was more joy and love in what we had and what we did than there had been in a while. The focus became enjoying our time together, sharing sentiments, and most of all being grateful for our health and each other.

The new year and newfound perspective brought phenomenal results. Opportunities began to surface where I was valuable for my knowledge and insight rather than my title. I could start contributing to worthwhile goals. Earning money became a result of helping people instead of a trade for my time. By the time COVID-19 engulfed our world in March of 2020, I was in full stride helping forge new healthcare delivery pathways. I was helping companies keep their employees safe while still at work providing for their families. While many people were quarantined at home "bored", I was busy helping the world evolve into a new reality as I had. I was emotionally and spiritually aligned with something fantastic. This evolution has been fast and exciting since its inception four and a half years ago. I look forward to experiencing its consistent benefits every single day.

**I wake up ready and excited to attack the day because I know I have the tools to grow through all experiences. This is the essence of freedom.**

When you wake up feeling confident, you will find that you are more connected with the world around you and the people in it. It feels enlightening and makes it easier to go out and face people because you recognize the value in what you have to offer—not in a financial sense but in a sense of general betterment to humankind.

Amazing things happen when you remain aligned mentally and spiritually. It is hard to evolve if you are not in alignment because in chaos opposing forces impede progress. Fear, which is a big theme in life, also lessens when you are aligned. You will know you are in alignment when you find meaning in everything you do.

## REFLECTIVE EXERCISES

A person who has evolved into their true self understands that their life is a product of their efforts in this world and what they draw from everyone they share the world with. The awareness that we are all connected and therefore can draw from collective knowledge is essential to optimize our evolutionary potential.

What you put into life can be gauged by evaluating the impact or contribution you have on your family, your peers, your community, and the world in general. Simple examples would include making sure your limited time with your kids is undivided and special every time, going out of your way to arrive to work on time so your colleague can leave on time and spend time with their family, giving a few hours of your time each month to a local charity, or simply picking up garbage at the local park or beach when you are on a walk.

Take some time to list the ways that you contribute. Don't be shy or too critical because these are fantastic ways to acknowledge that your contributions matter.

Now, let's reflect on connectivity with people in the world. This may feel harder to do, as it can trigger insecurities in yourself that make some connections uncomfortable. Realizing how our past experiences have impacted our ability to connect with others could be helpful.

Ponder this in your heart:

- Do you make an effort to listen to and understand all those you come in contact with?
- Do you avoid eye contact or engaging when you feel uncomfortable in a situation with others?
- Do you truly listen openly when in a conversation? Or do you find yourself making judgements while the other person is speaking?

- Do you learn something every time you have a conversation with someone? If the answer is no, there is a chance you were not truly listening. What could you be missing out on by not giving them the attention they deserve?
- Do you ever get the sense others don't seem to connect with you well? Why do you think that is? What are they missing out on by missing out on you?

It is easy to become self-involved with our thoughts. Sometimes we do this on purpose to avoid feelings and protect our ego. Don't miss out on the connectivity with all our fellow humans. It is only with their collective support that we can evolve into our best selves.

# WELCOME TO FREEDOM

"Freedom is the oxygen of the soul."

– MOSHE DAYAN

I like to think of it as the day I'll never forget, not because it was Thanksgiving but because of the call I received that day. The year was 2002, and just as I was preparing to carve the turkey, I received a call from my residency director. Even with a doctor's unusual hours, to receive a call on a holiday from my boss was unexpected. Without any small talk, or even a "Happy Thanksgiving" or "Sorry to bug you on a holiday," he started to voice his frustrations.

My boss told me that he had just spent an hour on the phone with the Director of Medicine at the VA hospital, a place where I had finished a rotation just a month earlier. Let's call this man Dr. G.

Dr. G was in his mid-to-late sixties, a veteran in the medical world with over thirty-five years of experience. I had no idea why the man would call my boss on Thanksgiving. I am not a psychic, but I had a feeling this phone call's intention was not to praise me.

The earful I got was nothing short of disturbing: Dr. G made it very clear to my boss that he felt personally insulted by me, although he could not provide specific reasons for feeling that way. My boss asked me what I had done to him, and I did not have a good answer. I honestly did not have any idea why or how I could have been such a nuisance to him and was at a loss for words.

The month I had spent in service at that VA hospital had been relatively smooth. However, Dr. G didn't care for me for his own mysterious reasons. I recall that during the first week as an intern in his service he was lecturing our team, when I had to leave the lecture to take care of a patient-related emergency. The very next morning Dr. G called me into the office before morning rounds at about 6am. He questioned my reasoning for leaving his obviously important lecture while he was in the middle of delivering it. When I explained that one of our patients needed emergency attention and I was summoned by the nursing staff, he dismissed my reasoning and began to question my integrity as a professional. From that day on, he made it a point to single me out in front of the entire team. His behavior toward me was obsessive and ridiculously unfair in my opinion. He also began to give me tasks that disrupted my days in what seemed like an effort to undermine my ability to meet my responsibilities to my patients. I admit that initially, I felt this was completely unfair, and I felt discriminated against in a sense. Luckily, I was able to compose myself and respond with integrity. I began to show up to the daily 5 am criticizing ceremony with a coffee in hand for Dr. G. I kept a soft smile on my face as he unloaded his criticism on me. I thanked him for the feedback and vowed to work on improving every single day. When he was done, I shook his hand and walked away with my head held high. I never disrespected him.

For that entire month, I chose to take that morning criticism and use it to fuel my resolve. I dove into work every day with a smile. I brought forth my best efforts to take care of patients, taught our medical students to the best of my ability, and treated all the staff like I would my family. Something about this made Dr. G even more irate with me. I am only human, and I admit I entertained the thought of punching the guy a time or two on his bulbous nose or just quitting. But I did neither. I brought him morning coffee with a bigger smile than ever, brushed off his morning insults (which had become a habit), and took on the extra workload he laid on me.

On Thanksgiving, nearly a month after I had finished my time in Dr. G's service, he called my residency director to discuss my evaluation. The comment that stood out to me on that evaluation was: "*Dr. Castillo simply seemed to be a day late and a dollar short.*" I just didn't understand why Dr. G had such a personal issue with me. Luckily my chief resident's review, which said I was the best intern he had ever worked with, allowed me to successfully pass that rotation. To this day I still don't know exactly what I did to insult Dr. G so gravely, although I have some theories!

Why is this story important? I like to share it because it cements the very purpose of this book. It reminds me that I can say all the right things, do everything expected of me, and excel in many ways and still be unappreciated, rejected, and even humiliated. The value comes from the lesson in that experience. I learned to accept criticism with dignity, evaluate the truth in that criticism, and use it to fuel my improvement. This story also serves as a reminder that I cannot please everyone all the time or always be liked, but never should I allow anyone to steer me off course.

**Life's difficult experiences and challenges are not mysteries that need to be solved; instead, they are lessons to grow from.**

Ultimately, this story embraces all the principles of this book and why I didn't let that experience define me. Instead, I chose to let it build me up. I am reminded that I am emotionally strong beyond belief, and my resolution to fulfill my purpose cannot waver even when I'm surrounded by uncertainty and disbelief.

At the heart of these 19 Principles are humans and the human experience. Today, I know the positivity and power that lie within these principles and how to use them for good.

- The hidden order of chaos guides you to sort out your emotional house, embracing your shortcomings and removing that which cannot serve your life well, liberates you.
- When discipline and integrity make up the foundation of your resolve, you will not waste time deliberating over any resistance in your path. With discipline and integrity, you will keep trying until you succeed!
- With a mind looking towards all the possibilities at your disposal, your excitement for life will never waiver, and you will forever continue to develop skills and qualities for progress toward any goal or undertaking that is important to you.

- By offering your best self to your work, you find dignity in every day's work even when the benefits are not so obvious. You will know because you will feel valued and strengthen your sense of purpose.
- Perseverance means never giving up, and it becomes a consequence of alignment when everything you are involved in is in tune with everything you are. You will wake up excited for the day ahead and you will keep making progress every single day of your life.
- Understanding your programming doesn't make you vulnerable. On the contrary, that knowledge gives you the foresight to make the necessary adjustments and capitalize on that programming. Don't ever forget that it is a choice to believe or not believe anything you are told.
- Being in alignment means that you are becoming more authentic and truer to yourself. Once you give yourself permission to be and accept yourself, staying rooted in your path is effortless and opens the way to life-defining opportunities. This leads to learning and growing in ways that are meaningful to you.
- Success is the progressive realization of an ideal goal. It stems from living your calling, not from any title you may hold or the amount of money you make. Success is something only you can define for yourself.
- You are part of a community whether you are aware of it or not. How you interact with that community or how much you contribute is directly correlated with the value that the community will reciprocate with. Becoming a pillar of your community will strengthen every aspect of your life and give you a sense of belonging, acceptance, and a sense of connection to what matters most in your life.
- *If you want to go fast, go alone. If you want to go far, go together.* -African proverb. An effective support network is the only

way to overcome challenges efficiently and effectively. Most everyone has a support network, even if they don't see it as one, but is yours composed to best serve your needs?

- Acceptance goes much beyond knowing who we are. Acceptance is about embracing everything that defines us—even those things that are undesirable. It is only when you know you are at point A that you can set course toward point B (your ideal goal!).

- The **quality** of being honest and having unwavering moral values is known as **integrity**. Which man or woman would not want to be known as a person of integrity? After all, without integrity there cannot be trust, and without trust all relationships fail.

- By being a student of life, for life, you are accepting that you are not perfect and never will be. You are telling yourself and the world that you are on a perpetual search for enlightenment, but never are you enlightened. This constant quest for growth, learning, and knowledge is the essence of freedom.

- Acts of courage never end in regret. Fear is what keeps most of us doing only what we can. Once you understand that you have the tools to conquer any challenges ahead, that fear to make mistakes disappears. If it doesn't completely disappear, you can at least tame it and move ahead despite it. In this life, take chances, DO WHAT YOU WANT! ONLY COWARDS DO WHAT THEY CAN.

Mastering your time is more about learning to say **NO** to a lot of opportunities that may sound fun or interesting. Prioritizing your goals and then dedicating your time in order of priority is a practice that will change your life. This practice will help you be mindful in all your tasks, dedicate uninterrupted time to all that matters, and feel fulfilled in everything you do.

- There is no such thing as unconditional love. You are not capable of loving without expectations so don't expect it in return. Instead, be clear about your needs and limits with all those you love. Listen and accept theirs as well. Love yourself as much as you do those closest to you, make that self-love obvious, and you will see how it becomes easier to accept love in all its forms and magnitudes.

- A pivot is not a failure. Being flexible and nimble allows for greater possibility of success. Remember from Principle 13 that you are a student of life, for life and therefore your beliefs and goals will forever be evolving. As you evolve, the pivot will become more frequent and more powerful. The ultimate goal is an ideal and therefore unattainable. This concept is so valuable it is worth repeating: "success is the progressive realization of a worthy ideal." The freedom to pivot is success!

- Transcendence is inevitable on the path you have chosen. Fear of transcending and losing touch with your community and even loved ones is a real possibility and therefore needs to be attacked directly like all other challenges. Bring those who can keep growing with you along on the journey and transcend all which do not serve your needs. When you take inventory, all those who truly matter will be at your side, not behind you.

- Evolving into the true you may simply be returning to that purity in which you were born. Accepting what you are and loving yourself for who you are makes it easy to be aligned in all aspects of life. Your authenticity attracts others on the same wavelength and path as yourself. This complete sense of alignment and peace offers that sense of freedom everyone in this world seeks. It is only in this freedom that we can finally live our life to its fullest potential.

## AS YOUR FREEDOM TAKES FLIGHT

As you read this book and worked through the reflective exercises, I hope you were reminded that your life, even when it has not gone as intended, has given you everything you needed. The fact you are still alive and reading this book means you are privileged. You've likely surpassed challenges and found ways to grow through those challenges. If I helped you extract more from each of your life's lessons as you relived your experiences, then the time I spent writing this book was worthwhile.

You are valuable, and this world does need you. Your insights and perspectives are unique. Just as sharing my lessons has helped you, yours could help others struggling to understand their journey.

Nobody will be a worse critic of yourself than you. Now that you have the insight to accept this criticism gracefully and grow from it, use that to be compassionate towards yourself and everyone you encounter. Immerse yourself in your community and the world at large better equipped to learn, love, and impact in any way you desire.

More than anything, after completing this book, I hope that you understand that your path to freedom may not be smooth and overlayed with a red carpet, and that's okay because you wouldn't want it any other way. You can now be sure that your path to freedom is specifically engineered to guide you to fulfill your purpose. I hope you know without a doubt that your freedom comes only when you have found alignment mentally, emotionally, physically, and spiritually. You have now become more grateful for the only thing that is real in the world, which is exactly everything you are in this moment.

Now it is time to put all you have learned to practice. Please don't forget that you are human and are not expected to be perfect. Know that some days, the path will be more difficult than others, but you have all the tools you need to conquer any challenge. Look forward to the unknown, for this is the only place where potential can be found! This is the freedom I live every day, and I wish the same for you.

May freedom reign.
Dr. Guillermo Castillo

# ABOUT THE AUTHOR

Dr. Guillermo Castillo is an expert in precision medicine with over twenty years of experience. This discipline of precision medicine takes the collective lessons from life circumstances, environmental factors, and genetic predispositions, then synthesizing these aspects of an individual to create a unique health plan—a health roadmap that will help the individual overcome their most difficult challenges. In essence, he helps people who want a better life health-wise to achieve it.

Guillermo comes from a humble background, a child of uneducated immigrant farmhands. The circumstances he was born into forced him to address potentially overwhelming situations from his youngest years onwards. Through managing these circumstances, he was able to draw strength and tenacity, extracting those experiences that forged an incredible fortitude and determination, along with the perseverance that led him to the success and freedom he now enjoys.

Today, Doctor Castillo lives in San Diego, California, where he raises his two teenage sons and enjoys fitness, travel, and satisfying his insatiable thirst for knowledge and information.